ecoescape®

Ire

Green travel begins here...

In memory of
Amanda Donegan

ecoescape®

Ireland

written by
Catherine Mack

edited by
Laura Burgess

GREENGUIDE

MARKHAM PUBLISHING • UNITED KINGDOM

Written by Catherine Mack and edited by Laura Burgess
Series art direction & cover design by Omaid Hiwaizi
ecoescape logo and responsible life cycle designed by Eskimo Design (www.eskimodesign.org.uk)
Research by Catherine Mack, Laura Burgess, Freda Palmer and Nuala Ryan

Cover image of Benbulben, Country Sligo © Catherine Mack
Unless otherwise indicated, or where images have been supplied by the businesses featured in
ecoescape, all original photos are copyright © Catherine Mack.

The ecoescape logo is a registered trade mark

This edition published May 2008 by Markham Publishing

ISBN 978-1-905731-29-9
Text copyright © 2008 Catherine Mack
Design copyright © Markham Publishing

Markham Publishing
31 Regal Road, Weasenham Lane Industrial Estate, Wisbech,
Cambridgeshire PE13 2RQ
United Kingdom
T: +44 (0) 1945 461 452
E: distribution@markhampublishing.co.uk
www.markhampublishing.co.uk

Printed and bound in the UK on FSC-certified, sustainable paper and board by Cambrian Printers Ltd,
Llanbadarn Road, Aberystwyth, Ceredigion SY23 3TN
T: +44 (0) 1970 613 000 E: info@cambrian-printers.co.uk W: www.cambrian-printers.co.uk

The views expressed in this guide are not necessarily those of the publishers.

Although we have tried to ensure the accuracy of the information provided in this book, the publishers
are not liable for any inaccuracies or inconvenience arising thereof.

Contents

ecoescape – the journey to Ireland

When a tall striking African man, dressed in traditional scarlet Maasai robes is in a room of besuited travel industry heads, he certainly stands out. When he stops the UN representative in his tracks during the Q&A session of a lecture on sustainable tourism by saying, "All we want is a voice", he thankfully brings the debate to life. It was a wake up call for me anyway. It was 2006, and I was in the middle of a Masters degree in Responsible Tourism Management when I heard this Maasai warrior speak passionately about trying to get tourists to understand their culture, why they needed to find sustainable fuel sources and how they were being driven off their land so that tourists could shoot lions. Digitally, of course. At this time, I was already thinking of trying to incorporate some of the issues I had been studying around sustainable tourism into a more consumer-friendly medium. The Maasai voice stayed in my head, and I started to write.

I then undertook, for my Masters research, an extensive study of the UK travel media to see whether they were including any of the issues of responsible tourism in their travel articles. This research was 40,000 words long. But it could be summarised in two. Not really. So, the door was open, I started to pitch responsible travel ideas to the same editors I had just criticised. Some of them kindly took me on, and others said no thanks. "Our readers don't like it when writers are too 'worthy'", one paper told me. "No moral high ground, please", was another. "Too niche", was the usual response. So, worthiness kept safely at bay, I stepped down off my high horse, and tried to just write about the (eco)places I loved, why I loved them, and why I thought 'non-nichers' might love them too. It seems to have worked so far.

This has led me back to Ireland, my home country. One of my first articles was about 'green tourism' in Northern Ireland, for an English newspaper. During this trip, I met several of the people I feature in this book, one of whom was Marella Fyffe, owner of The Omagh Hostel, one of the greenest hostels in Ireland. She told me, "Quite honestly, we will just have to close soon, if we can't fill the beds. It's just too hard. How does somewhere like my hostel get to be known out there in the world?" She was as direct in expressing her frustrations as the Maasai.

I am glad to say that I did go on to write about Marella and the Maasai man. I do not claim to have made a huge difference to their lives at all. Far from it. They are the ones doing all the amazing work. Building houses, digging land for reed beds, rearing animals, welcoming visitors into their homes, cutting down trees and planting more, storytelling, creating communities, and sharing a pride in their culture with a generosity of spirit which is typical of many of the people I have had the honour of meeting. The only thing that I do is try and tell people about them, their stories and the places they live in. I have tried to avoid being over-worthy. It hasn't always worked. I am much more guilty, however, of being over-wordy. I am extremely grateful to my editor, Laura Burgess, who had faith and allowed me to do my thing. So here they are. Fifty voices. Fifty ecoescapes. ■

Catherine Mack
May 2008
www.ecoescape.org

Ballintoy, County Antrim © britainonview/Martin Brent

Passing the Irish test

When you go to a restaurant in another country, the guidebooks always tell you to check out if the locals eat there. That's a good sign, apparently.

I hope, most importantly therefore, that people living in Ireland will read ecoescape. If they do, and they like it, then visitors might follow suit. Because this book is all about going local. It is part of the worldwide responsible tourism movement, which is reassessing the impacts of tourism on destinations we love to visit. Is tourism having negative impacts on the Irish environment? Is it providing an income for Irish residents? Is tourism sustaining Ireland's cultural make-up?

Few Irish people travelling at home want to damage their own environment. Everyone wants to keep their own economy as strong as possible. And I don't know any Irish people who go in search of leprechauns. So, rather selfishly, being Irish, I wanted to write a guidebook for me. And for my friends. To share the stories of great people who are, quite simply, trying to make a difference. They are striving to make a living out of Irish tourism, but taking responsibility for the impacts it might have locally. These are the sort of people I like to meet wherever I travel in the world. Meeting them in my own home country was an added bonus. I hope some of the other Irish people who take regular trips at home might like to meet them too. And if they pass the Irish test, then that's a good sign, isn't it? ■

Don't mention the war

I lived in Dublin for eight years, where the first topic of conversation is usually, "where are you from?" It's not a test; it's just one of the things they do to make conversation and because they want to know, and are interested.

I say 'they' because I am from Belfast, and when I was growing up there in the 70's and 80's, I dreaded being asked "where are you from?" I never knew what the right answer should be. It carried too much political baggage. In fact, it was often a question on people's lips, but the very question one never dared to ask.

It is impossible to avoid politics when writing a travel book, especially in Ireland. In the early days of researching it, there were many questions. Do we cover North and South? Do we call it ecoescape Ireland, or do we include Northern Ireland in the UK edition? If we mention the 'government', do we need to specify the British or Irish one? Don't mention bombs. Don't mention the war. However, ecoescape Ireland is political. It has to be, because tourism is about people just as much as it is about places. By trying to promote a more ethical form of tourism, we are, like it or not, being political. The difference is that this book is not about borders. If you are visiting Ireland, you will quickly discover that the beauty does not stop at the border. Yet Northern Ireland struggled to get tourism back on its feet until very recently, due to visitors' fear of violence. I can understand that, I couldn't get out of Belfast quickly enough when I was eighteen.

Writing this book has not only allowed me to discover Northern Ireland again, but also to remind myself that the mountains don't stop at the border. Take yourself to the top of Slieve Foy in County Louth, and you will see that Carlingford Lough is the only physical divide between you and the other peaks in the Mourne mountain range across the water in Northern Ireland. The lakelands of the North West flow peacefully between Fermanagh, Leitrim and Cavan, and the rugged coastline doesn't stop at Donegal or Dundalk, because of a blue line that goes through it on the map. And yet cross-border tourism, particularly from South to North, is still resistant to this notion. Try Strangford Lough in County Down as an appetizer, Fermanagh as a main course, and Rathlin Island in County Antrim for dessert, and I guarantee all preconceptions will be shattered. ■

A green Ireland?

During the research for the book, many people told me I would never find fifty ecoescapes in Ireland. These were the usual reasons given; Ireland isn't ready. There are too many cars on the road. It's an island, so everyone has to fly there. The Celtic Tiger has made tourism all about targets. Budget flights have turned Ireland into a citybreak destination.

Some of these are true, of course. But there is a flipside to all of these arguments. Ireland is pretty progressive in terms of environmental policies. The Green Party agreed to enter a coalition government in 2007. Fáilte Ireland, the Irish tourist board, has appointed a proactive Environmental Manager. The Slow Food Movement is huge and the national food board, Bord Bia, has created a label for restaurants which promotes sustainable food sourcing. There has been a virtual elimination of plastic bags since there was a tax introduced on them in 2002. Greenbox, the ecotourism organisation based in the North West (see pages 61-62), has received international accolades for its work towards creating an ecotourism destination in the North West of Ireland.

ecoescape Ireland is not about 'them and us'. Tourism is a business, and a hugely important one for countries like Ireland. Seeing responsible tourism kick into the mainstream market in Ireland is very exciting. ecoescape Ireland aims to play a small role in this bigger picture of a changing Ireland, where sustainability is starting to seep into the very core of all industries, not just tourism.

So, we did find fifty, and many more. Some are at different stages of discovering the advantages of becoming green. There are still more out there being created at the time of publication, and I hope this book provides a little encouragement to those people. And I look forward to visiting them the next time around.

See pages 24-25 for an overview of 50 of Ireland's best ecoescapes ■

Catherine and family.

Friends and family

Researching this book was one of the most wonderful times of my life. The only downside was that I didn't ever seem to get enough time in each ecoescape, whether it was a shop, shebeen or shelter. However, this made choosing our ecoescapes easy. If it left me wanting more, then it was in.

I also made some wonderful new friends among those who hosted me. One man's mother had just had a severe stroke, and yet he insisted on taking my children out in the canoe after a long day at the hospital, and did so with a smile on his face. Touching gestures such as daffodils from the garden being left on the doorstep, with a note saying 'Catherine, you are so very welcome'. I was staying at Blaney Spa when I heard of the death of a very close friend. Gabriele, the owner, made me tea and gave me a massage. My children, Louis and Hugo, got to sit on the Connemara pony at Cnoc Suain and, with the gentle guidance of the owners, Dearbhaill and Charlie, they overcame a fear of dogs. A few weeks later, the dogs and pony even sent the boys a Happy St. Patrick's Day card. In Enniskillen I raved to one of my hosts about the venison steaks I had bought at the nearby famous O'Doherty's butchers, only to find the next day that two packets of his sublime "Black Bacon" had been slipped into my bag to take home. One family was taking its time moving out of Crom Cottage, on the day that I was meant to be moving in. They come every year without fail, and this time it was a family reunion. The owner, Damien, hadn't the heart to hurry them into packing their bags, so he took me to his family home for lunch. We all hung out for a while, watched the rugby, and shared a glass or two. The stories go on and on.

Ireland may be changing, but the ability to welcome visitors in an open, relaxed and uncomplicated way, is here to stay. It's not a cliché. It's just part of the Irish make-up. As you go out there and meet them all, you too will get a chance to chat with these people and hear about their ventures into tourism. Most of these are dream projects which they have worked towards for years, and some are still battling against bureaucratic, financial or personal obstacles to fully realise them. I hope that ecoescape spreads the word for them, and accurately describes what these people, some now good friends, have achieved. ■

"I have spread my dreams beneath your feet; tread softly because you tread on my dreams" WB Yeats

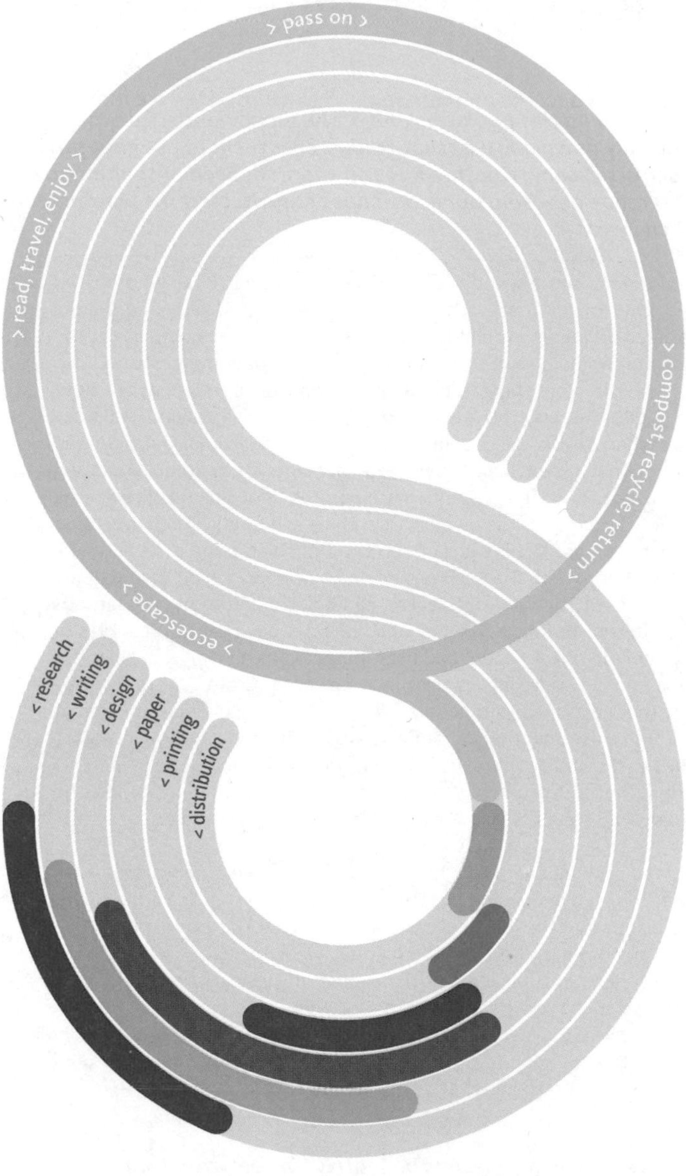
> pass on >
> compost, recycle, return >
> ecoescape >
> read, travel, enjoy >
< research
< writing
< design
< paper
< printing
< distribution

ecoescape's responsible life cycle

The responsible life cycle

For ecoescape, the medium really is the message. Like most people we're not perfect but we try to keep the responsible life cycle (left) at the centre of everything we do, ensuring the book and our business tread as carefully as you do.

The responsible life cycle is a way of recognising that our actions, no matter how big or small, have an impact on the environment. When we put together the first edition of ecoescape, we knew that along with a message to help travellers go green, it was crucial to be respectful of the resources we needed to produce a guidebook. We've continued this mantra into the production of this book and subsequent editions in the series. In the responsible life cycle, the reader also takes responsibility for the impact of the guide through recycling, sharing and composting. And so the cycle continues.

The responsible life cycle is also a metaphor. It helps keep our travels grounded because it reminds us that travel is about the impact of an entire trip. That means from our home, through a journey to a destination and back home again. ecoescape not only offers inspiration but also encourages you to share your stories of responsible escapism. People have been sharing stories about travel since pre-history. Storytelling has helped humans survive, protect and enjoy their environment and that's why we hope you will feel inspired to share your experiences with others at **www.ecoescape.org**.

How did we make this book?

Research: We hopped on trains, buses, bicycles, bio-taxis and, of course, used our legs. See our Slow Travel Tool Kit on page 151 for our advice on how to get around Ireland without a car or plane.

Energy: Website and computers powered by the wind, see **www.green-hosting.co.uk** and **www.ecotricity.co.uk**

Print: We use a printer in Wales. They have won numerous awards for their green printing, collect water from the roof for their presses, only use FSC-certified papers and boards and even have a wormery under the stairs for their organic waste. The book is printed on 100% recycled paper using vegetable-based inks. ∎

Getting off-grid: home

'Home is where one starts from.' TS Eliot

You may wonder why we talk about home in a guide that's about travel and getting away. ecoescape begins at home. It's about reconnecting to familiar places – our cities, villages, birthplace or countries – and finding ways to escape that we may never have realised were there.

We also want you to discover new spaces to think and breathe. ecoescape helps you find ways to get off-grid at home and further afield without sacrificing the quality of travel experience or the potential to relax and escape everyday life.

We think of an ecoescape as our getting-off-grid way of being. Whether you see home as something that is (pretty much) fixed, a metaphor or even a transitional place to lay your head and stash your belongings, home is a space for dwelling and disconnecting from the stresses of life and work. Often this is an idea, not a reality. This means finding ways to escape are important, if not essential! We call this process getting 'off-grid', both mentally and physically in a way that also reduces the impact of our travels on the environment. That's why our ecoescape suggestions are forms of responsible escapism; they minimise the impact on the planet's resources and offer a more sustainable approach to getting-off-grid when we travel. From experience we know that when we then return home we feel more inspired to integrate sustainable ways of living into our everyday lives.

We think that the greenest travel options for ecoescaping are on our doorstep not only because we'll be reducing our carbon emissions by travelling closer to home but also because the choice for green places to stay and visit in Ireland is growing by the day. The recommendations in ecoescape take into account the environmental cost of our travel bug and are real ways to reduce the impact we have on the environment. ■

Getting there slowly: the journey

We need the earth to see the earth. No matter how hard we try, we'll never separate the environment from travel. It is at the centre of every trip we make. It gives us the energy to reach our destination, however near or far and often we get the desire to travel in order to experience a different environment.

But how much longer can we afford to neglect thinking about the transition that takes us from A to B? It's often the part of the holiday we least look forward to. In fact we've also become adept at maximising our distance and minimising the costs of travelling. By doing so, we've developed an ostrich-like approach in ignoring the effects of travel. We make excuses for taking flights when a train could suffice. We tell ourselves one journey won't matter as we jump in the car when walking could be possible. If we were to look at the journey before deciding on the destination, just think how different our experiences would be and how much easier it is to take the environment into consideration.

Slow travellers are now rekindling a sense of adventure in an always-on, globally interconnected and 'I can get (pretty much) anywhere on the planet within 24 hours' kind of world. The boundaries of slow travel are being explored by those avoiding airports and motorways.

Travelling slowly overland anywhere in the world is becoming a way of harnessing the journey so that what we see on the way is as important as what we do when we arrive. And that's why you'll find details of public transport and ways to arrive at the ecoescape destinations without using a car or a plane. As we've tried and tested many of these ideas, we're able to prove that it's possible.

We know that ecoescaping will take some people a while to understand. But with gradual changes we think it is possible to introduce new ways of thinking about travel that will lead to long-lasting lifestyle changes. There would be no sense in creating a guide that tried to save you time and money while promoting the needs of the environment and planet. When we've dealt with these questions, suddenly the desire to squeeze ourselves onto a 1p flight to 'save' time, or tick off 'must-see' boxes declines. In doing so we have found people come to think of how their lives are a part of a bigger story we are all writing about and how our actions (big and small) ripple outward. ecoescape is all about making these ripples happen by ensuring our journeys have a positive impact.

Turn to page 151 to consult our Slow Travel Tool Kit for more advice and slow travel tips. ∎

How green do we go?

One of the most frequently asked questions is 'how does ecoescape decide which businesses to include in the book?' The next few pages will explore the thinking behind what we include in our guides.

None of the businesses have paid to be included in the book. Nor do we get paid commission for every holiday you book using ecoescape. We keep our editorial decisions independent from commercial ones. Although many of the businesses have received formal awards for their green initiatives, ecoescape has another set of requirements which are difficult to measure. We look for businesses that demonstrate that along with fulfilling the criteria set by green accreditation schemes and government initiatives, they offer innovative ways of involving their customers in the travel experience. The business owners need to offer guests an insight into the local communities that sustain them through their supplies of energy, food, drink, local crafts and expertise.

An ecoescape is about what the destination offers as an experience and a way to get 'off-grid'. In other words the business has to add to the stock of stories about responsible escapism. The ecoescape suggestions in this guide therefore contribute to a storybook of how the owners think travel is possible whilst also paying respect to the natural environment in which they live and welcome others to stay.

We've also found that businesses do not adopt a like-for-like approach to sustainability. By the very nature of sustainability, business owners find that they have to adapt to their surroundings to ensure their patch of the environment is protected. This could be looking out for the local wildlife or using a renewable natural resource to generate energy. So the businesses featured in this book each have a story that connects the founders' biographies and the direction of their business to the local environments they have chosen to inhabit, protect and invite others to experience.

ecoescape uses four main criteria to map how a business in the tourism industry reduces its impact on the environment. These are: conservation, energy, waste and food. Under these headings there are numerous ways a business can improve its environmental performance. All of the business owners in ecoescape take each area seriously and they'll opt for various ways to deal with these areas, carefully using, renewing or micro-generating resources obtainable in a specific location. Of course there is a lot of variation too. Some

Mourne Mountains, County Down

business owners might grow their own produce; generate energy through solar panels; encourage use of public transport, offer an honesty shop, or invest in ingenious ways of recycling waste.

Once we're convinced that all measures possible are taken by the business owners we want to make sure the experiences they offer are attractive. This doesn't necessarily mean that every room should have a widescreen TV, tea-making facilities or a trouser press. We look for places and destinations that not only have a strong environmental commitment but incorporate all their responsible escapism credentials into an experience that shouldn't put customers off. After all, no one likes being preached to, especially when they are on holiday. ■

Case study: Ard Nahoo
Dromahair, County Leitrim

Noeleen Tyrrell and Brendan Murphy moved into Ard Nahoo in County Leitrim in 1994. Here we map out their journey to realising their dream of setting up an ecoescape in Dromahair.

- Noeleen and Brendan move to Dromahair from Dublin, so Noeleen can join a band. (1994)

- They buy 6 acres above Loch Nahoo which includes an old house (three walls) and a dilapidated barn. (1994)

- Noeleen starts a holistic therapy business in Sligo as the house is being converted.

- They build a small office on site in which Noeleen can conduct treatments, as the first baby is due. (1999)

- The barn is converted into a health farm in order to accommodate more clients, including a Green Room used for yoga classes, two treatment rooms, a floatation tank and steam room. (2001)

- Ard Nahoo hosts the first ever Green Living Festival (2003)

- A small cabin is built to accommodate residential stays. The Wise Women festival is held at Ard Nahoo (2005)

- Noeleen and Brendan research different sustainable architects in order to develop Ard Nahoo. They hire Peter Cowman of Living Architecture who proposes they 'expand to contract', with the extra facets of the business demanding less time than the present health farm. (2006)

- The grounds are developed to include a wild flower meadow, wildlife pond and Celtic Nature Trail. (2007)

- The health farm is closed in order to build two Eco Cabins, a new yoga studio and the Uisce Area, an indoor/outdoor wet area with sauna and hot tub. The entire construction was conducted with green principles, and all buildings are timber-framed, cedar-cladded, finished with natural paints, heated with pellet stoves with limited concrete and no petro chemicals. (2007)

- Ard Nahoo is awarded the EU Flower, the only sign of environmental quality both certified by an independent organisation and valid throughout Europe (2007).

- The new Ard Nahoo is opened by John Gormley, leader of the Green Party. (2008)

- The Eco Cabins are given their first run with a venue hire booking for a yoga teacher training weekend (2008).

- Groups can be picked up by Ireland Ecotours, with bus run on vegetable oil.

- Bike hire can be arranged for visitors.

- Organic vegetable box can be ordered in advance for visitors.

- Venue can be rented for retreats, courses, corporate events or groups (small weddings, family reunions etc).

- Organic herb gardens planted between Eco Cabins.

To read more about Ard Nahoo, turn to page 82.

Bellinter House, County Meath.

How green do you go?

ecoescape will never compromise on comfort or quality of escapism. Of course luxury is a question of taste and for some people it might mean spending the weekend doing what they love doing, like surfing or simply relaxing with friends and family and eating good food. An ecoescape business must facilitate the everyday things we already love doing together with environmentally-friendly infrastructures and activities that compliment, but tend not to become the foreground of a travel experience. We promote quality experiences at the centre of every ecoescape.

Now tell your story

Don't forget that the strength of the force to bring about changes to the way we travel is partly reliant on you telling your stories of responsible escapism to others. So please visit our website at **www.ecoescape.org** and tell the businesses, other escapers and us what you think about our selection. You can always contact us with your own ecoescapes as well.

Our email address is **tellyourstory@ecoescape.org** ■

50 of Ireland's best ecoescapes

The North West

Northern Ireland

The West

The East

The Midlands

The South East

The South West

The West

National Organisations

"Tree Sentinels" by Susan O'Toole at South Reen Farm, County Cork.

the South West

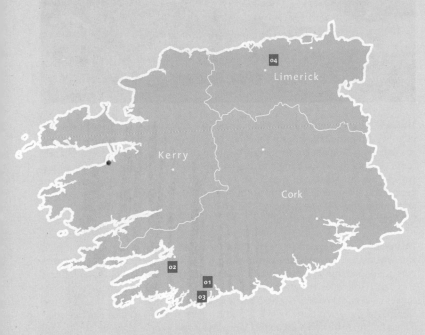

The website calls it a retreat. I call it a rural idyll. It is so peaceful here that when I strolled from the house down the lane to the tiny sandy cove, I wanted to test the echo and shout 'hello'. Or hurray. Because this place epitomises ecoescape's remit. A modern self-catering house on Ann Shaw's remote organic farm, where you can buy the slowest of slow food: Ann's own organic vegetables, meat from her organically reared cattle, and produce from local farmers' markets are within a few kilometres. The best one is Skibbereen 13km away, where the South Reen Beef stall is one to look out for.

This place is surrounded by water. From the dark green waters of Reen pier, where you can take a whale watching trip with local experts (see Whale Watch West Cork on page 33), and beyond that to the tiny cove at South Reen itself. This beach is lined with sycamore trees, and there is enough slate on the rocky shores to keep skimmers in stock for eternity. After a quick dip I ran back to the warmth of the wood-burning stove, and a hot shower, heated by the five solar panels (with a little back up, I admit). Anne plants and coppices trees, so all wood is from a sustainable source, water is from the local well, and the peace is free of charge too.

Take a stroll over the hill to be hit by the full-on surge of the Atlantic. Reputed to be one of the first areas struck by the Famine, Ann commissioned a sculpture to commemorate those lost from this townland. "Tree Sentinels" by Susan O'Toole (on page 26) is a work of mammoth proportions. Eighteen wooden poles,

t: +353 (0) 28 33258
w: www.southreenfarm.com

standing 27 feet high, shake in the wind at the top of the cliff, almost keening for those who took refuge on the seas.

The décor is cream, white and wood. No other colours are necessary, with the ever-changing natural colourscapes on full show. It sleeps nine, so you can bring a clatter of kids to test the echos and skim stones from dawn until dusk. Ann is not precious about her 'retreat'. All are welcome.

Contact details
Address: South Reen Farm, Union Hall, County Cork
Telephone: +353 (0) 28 33258
Website: www.southreenfarm.com
Price: €650-1,050 per week, depending on season
Opening times: All year round
Disabled access: Full access, with bedrooms on ground floor as well as first floor. Both downstairs bedrooms are ensuite with disabled shower in one. The lane leads right down to the beach for easy access by car

Getting there slowly
The nearest mainline railway station is Cork, 50km from South Reen where you can get a bus to Skibbereen, 13km from South Reen. Ann has three bikes available for visitors, but you can also hire them in Skibbereen. Call Roycroft Cycles, +353 (0)28 21235, for details.

Drink at Dinty's
Union Hall has one shop and five pubs. Hopefully you will have a chance to sample all of them, but the fish pie was Dinty's prize dish the night of my visit. Guinness is beautifully settled too. Huge platefuls of food, with generous half portions of all main meals for children. For dessert, plump for the lumpy bumpy chocolate pie. This is the only pub I have seen a grown man wash his dinner down with a pint of milk. So the milk must be pretty good too.
Address: Dinty's Bar, Union Hall, County Cork
Telephone: +353 (0) 28 33373

My hosts, Janny and Fred, greeted me with herbal tea which looked like a work of art. A glass jug on a candle warmer, gently infusing home-grown fennel, liquorice root, cardamom and an apple. A rose perfectly poised on the jug's brim. This sums up Hagal Farm. Everything here embraces nature, simple beauty and natural healing.

There is something almost fairy-like about this hideaway in the hills overlooking Bantry Bay. The entrance to the main house is via a rose covered stone staircase, past a burgeoning herb garden and signs to 'the labyrinth'. The separate entrance to the bedrooms is hobbitesque. It leads to four rooms, all leading in turn to a mystical spiral staircase. Hand-made by Fred from local wood, it takes you past the sauna to a communal sitting room in the attic. The crystals and candles illuminating this space kept my feet firmly in fairy land.

My room was modestly furnished, warm and comfy, with fresh flowers, candles and hot water bottles by the bed. Not that I needed one, with the efficient solar

t: +353 (0) 27 66179
w: www.hagalholistichealth.com

powered underground heating. The ensuite loo led down to a reed bed, and all water is sourced from the river and nearby well.

Food here is made by a god, not the fairies. Fred's freshly made scones at breakfast will have you booking a place on his cookery weekend. I opted for dinner as well, and could not have found finer fare this side of the Ring of Kerry. Organic vegetarian cuisine at its best. Served in a vine-covered conservatory, with the grapes almost willing to land on your cheese plate. Coffee was served in the living room, a den of warmth emanating not only from the roaring fire, but from the very fabric of this house.

You can opt for one of many holistic treatments or book a healing weekend such as massage, detox or reflexology. Or just sit back, and see what the fairies have in store for you. No one will try to read your aura if that is not your thing. But I defy anyone to leave this haven not feeling better about themselves.

Contact details

Address: Hagal Farm,
Coomleigh West, Bantry, West Cork
Telephone: +353 (0) 27 66179
Website:
www.hagalholistichealth.com
Price: B&B €35 per person sharing.
Full board €70 per person sharing.
Self-catering house in the garden
€100-125 per night (sleeps 6-7)
Opening times: All year round
Disabled access: The new self-catering
facilities have disabled access, but
the main house is up a rocky staircase

Getting there slowly

Take a train to Cork, and there are six
buses a day from Cork to the nearest
town of Bantry. Situated about 11 kilometres from Bantry, you can take a cab
to the farm, or if Janny or Fred are in
town, they are happy to collect visi-
tors. There are two mountain bikes for visitors who want to tackle the
surrounding hills.

Visit the islands

There is a wide variety to choose from off these rugged coasts such as Dursey
Island, accessible only by cable car (more like a shed on wires) from Ballaghboy,
on the tip of the Beara peninsula. Whiddy Island, a short boat ride from Bantry,
has the bizarre juxtaposition of an oil terminal on one side, and quiet coves on
the other. Or Bere (sometimes called Bear) Island, accessible from Pontoon, near
Castletownbere where, if you cycle all the way around, you can have an archae-
ological feast of Victorian military fortifications, standing stones and ring forts.
For excellent information on all islands, see www.irelandsislands.com.

Drink at Ma Murphy's

Ma Murphy's bar in Bantry is one of Ireland's few untouched pubs with a shop
in the front. Have lunch at Organico Café, with superb bakery wholefood shop.
Enjoy Friday night music with Spanish food at El Gitano, both in Bantry. If you
can face leaving Fred's cooking, that is.
Address: Organico, 2 Glengarriff Road, Bantry, County Cork
Telephone: +353 (0) 27 51391
Website: www.organico.ie

Don't get Nic Slocum onto the subject of jet skis. He will see red. Hard for a man who lives for all that is green. A marine zoologist and conservationist, he gave up city life to share his greatest love with the world. In his bespoke whale watching catamaran, RV Voyager, he takes small groups of tourists from the tiny Reen pier in Castlehaven harbour into the West Cork waters. On a good day you can see Minke, Fin, or Humpback whales, as well as the ever faithful Bottle-Nosed or Common Dolphins. On a bad day, well you can't have one of those with Nic at the helm. His knowledge of marine wildlife, and his passion for educating young and old, is uplifting from the minute you board.

This is a four-hour trip, so not for the weak-stomached. But the spray from a Fin Whale blown against the deep dark waters of the Atlantic is the most exhilarating way to combat sea sickness. I was impressed to see that children and adults are given lifejackets to wear, despite the fact that they are not legally obliged to wear them. I didn't see anyone mess with Nic's firm delivery of safety and conservation instructions. "I don't chase a whale just for a photo. I know the limits of each creature, and they vary from one species to another, so I judge accordingly".

Whale Watch West Cork's website is informative and up to date, with daily news on sightings and excellent information on all species. They have a viewing success rate of between 82-85% and, depending on the time of year, you can see a variety of species during one trip. Minke Whales tend to appear in May, Fin Whales arrive in late June and can stay for up to seven months, and you

t: +353 (0) 28 33357
w: www.whalewatchwestcork.com

may be lucky enough to catch a viewing of a Humpback Whale between September and November.

Nic's expertise has led him to draw up a Code of Conduct for Whale Watching, to encourage best practice in conservation and education in the whale watching business. Let's hope all other operators follow suit. That should keep those jet skiers at bay.

Contact details
Address: Whale Watch West Cork, Carrigillihy, Union Hall, County Cork
Landline: +353 (0) 28 33357 (mobile +353 (0) 86 120 0027)
Website: www.whalewatchwestcork.com
Price: For 3-4 hour trip, €50 per person
Opening times: Trips between April and November. In the early season, trips at 10am and 2pm. Peak season trips at 5.30am, 9am and 2pm
Disabled access: No disabled access

Getting there slowly
The nearest mainline railway station is Cork, 50km away. From here take the bus to Skibbereen, where you can hire a bike at Roycroft Cycles (telephone +353 (0) 28 21235 for details) which is about 6km from Union Hall.

Go Kayaking
If you find it hard to leave the dark green waters of this exquisite harbour, then you can keep going until the sun sets. Local kayaker Jim Kennedy, of Atlantic Sea Kayaking, takes groups midnight kayaking off Reen pier. He also does half day and full day excursions, as well as week-long courses. But going out at night, and watching the phosphorescence, which almost seems to dance on the water, is an experience not to be missed. As for Jim, he is one of those guys who will make you stop paddling, in the middle of a dark pier, and close your eyes. Just to listen to the night time happening all around you. That way, you will take the memory with you, he says. This is kayaking, Jim, but not as we know it.
Address: Reen Pier, Union Hall, West Cork
Telephone: +353 28 21058
Website: www.atlanticseakayaking.com

Churches and chapels have become one of the more unpredictable themes in ecoescape. This is due to the conversion of many of their buildings for tourism. Echo Lodge was once the Mercy Sisters' Convent, built in 1884, and now the home to one of County Limerick's finest country hotels and restaurants. These precious buildings are an important part of Ireland's heritage, and it's thanks to people like Dan Mullane, the owner, that many of them are being preserved and shared with visitors.

The Mustard Seed restaurant was originally in nearby Adare, but its fine reputation and popularity led to it being replanted at Echo Lodge in nearby Ballingarry. With its ten acres of mature trees and gardens, and lush green lawns, there was plenty of room to expand the restaurant business into a truly resplendent country manor. There is nothing of the stark convent about the building now. Its soft yellow exterior glows invitingly at the top of its laneway. The bedrooms are furnished with richly coloured fabrics and some have four poster beds. The library, which catches the early morning sun through its great bay windows, towers over the lawns and Ballingarry in the distance.

I loved the quirky collection of trinkets from around the world, contemporary and antique. Many of these are Dan's souvenirs from years of travelling; sepia prints of cherubs, black and white pictures of ancient Greece and Rome and a barrage of Buddha's sitting on the mantelpiece. It was also a first to see works of art from the brushes of the hotel employees on the walls. Dan's travels have taught him all about maintaining a policy of sustainability at Echo Lodge. He doesn't apologise for reminding guests, with polite notes, to turn off lights or conserve water. They recycle everything, 'Not even an egg-shell goes un-recycled', said Dan. Strolling around the gardens there are little signs of this

t: +353 (0) 69 68508
w: www.mustardseed.ie

everywhere. Barrels left under roof gutters for rainwater, or wooden pallets reused to create compost heaps.

Trees that are cut down for firewood are replaced, and the Nun's Walk, where the Mercy Sisters once walked to say the Rosary, now leads to a kitchen garden heaven. Here, Dan invites guests to help themselves to some fresh lemon verbena, fennel or mint and prepare their own herbal tea to sip in the library. These gardens and orchard, which provide the hotel with a high level of self-sufficiency, would be the answer to many gardeners' prayers.

Contact details
Address: The Mustard Seed at Echo Lodge, Ballingarry, County Limerick
Telephone: +353 (0) 69 68508
Website: www.mustardseed.ie
Price: B&B from €95-165 per person sharing
Opening times: All year round
Disabled Access: Full disabled access, with ramps providing access to the hotel and a designated bedroom to cater for wheelchair users

Getting there slowly
Take the train to Charleville, and then taxi or cycle 24km. Very limited bus service to Ballingarry, but regular buses to Adare (8km) or Rathkeale (12km).

Walk the Knockfierna
The Nun's Walk to 'The Hill of Truth' is the favourite local walk, otherwise known as Knockfierna. It climbs to height of 286 metres, and has always been considered a sacred place. Celtic myth has it as the place of worship to Donn Firinne, Celtic god to the Otherworld. More recently, locals who were evicted from their homes in the famine times of 1840s, fled to these slopes to live in simple mud huts, and many starved to death. You can see remains of some of these huts, some partially restored.

the South East

I like a place that doesn't have lots of notes and instructions stuck up everywhere. There were only two notes when I arrived at this tiny white stone cottage. One on the door from Eamonn, the farmer who created this eco gem, which says, "door open, put timber in fire", and another pegged to the lightswitch giving us stove lighting instructions, the last of which reads, "Wash hands after handling timber". Worthwhile advice from the man who farms the land all around, as there is a risk of catching ringworm from timber.

This cottage was an experiment. Ten years ago, the powers that be were offering funding to find ways of getting tourists off the Ring of Kerry and into the rest of rural Ireland. Eamonn received funding to rebuild his disused cottage but keep it as 'natural' as possible. This he took literally. He installed a water

t: +353 (0) 52 65191
w: www.ecobooley.com

turbine feeding off the local mountain stream to generate electricity, a wood-burning stove using wood from the land, built furniture using spent oak, sought out natural mattresses filled with recycled clothing, used organic paints, local tweed curtains, insulated the roof with sheep's wool and plastered the walls with lime and hemp.

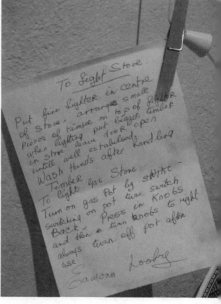

This was before green became the new black, and it was a challenge. Especially to comply with the official self-catering standards which had not, at the time, found a 'box' to put EcoBooley into. But despite such bodies insisting on 'matching crockery, because that is what tourists want these days', this is still a real ecoescape, with no sign of chrome or corian. If you don't mind rough and ready, rattling pipes, an old kettle on the stove, and chats with the wonderfully affable and knowledgeable Eamonn about water temperature regulation or renewable energy, this is the perfect budget green getaway. Especially for walkers and families. Sleeping five, you can stick on the cleverly supplied slowcooker in the morning, then your boots, and walk straight out the front door into the forests and foothills of the Knockmealdown Mountains, part of the East Munster Way (see www.walkireland.ie for details).

Contact details

Address: EcoBooley, Ronga, Clogheen, County Tipperary
Telephone: +353 (0) 52 65191 (best time to call, 7-9pm)
Website: www.ecobooley.com
Price: From €130 for a weekend to €350 for a week in high season
Opening times: All year round
Disabled access: Not accessible for wheelchairs

Getting there slowly

Take a bus from Cork to Clogheen, or train to Cahir (12km) or Clonmel (27km). Phone Eamonn to arrange a cab or collection. There is a very efficient local service called Ring a Link. Operating Fridays and Saturdays only, ring 1890 42 41 41 (internally only) to get a bus direct from EcoBooley to Clonmel and back (adult return €5). Perfect to catch the Saturday Organic Market (Anglesea St) and Farmers' Market (Kickham St) both in Clonmel.

Eat at the Old Convent

What's lacking in local hostelries is made up for in local food suppliers. One of the finest is award-winning Baylough Farm, a walk up the hill from Clogheen. Anne, the farmer turned cheese-maker, is the only licensed producer of Irish cheddar (telephone +353 (0) 52 65275 for directions). Other local producers worth a visit are the Apple Farm, Moorstown, Cahir and William's Honey in Tincurry. One restaurant making the most of all this fine produce, and you will need to hide your muddy boots in the car for this one, is the Old Convent, on the outskirts of Clogheen. Booking is advisable and the restaurant is open from Thursday to Sunday only.

Address: The Old Convent, Mount Anglesby, Clogheen, County Tipperary
Telephone: +353 (0) 52 65565
Website: www.theoldconvent.ie

Walk the Tipperary Heritage Trail

Walk a section or two of the Tipperary Heritage Trail nearby – a total of 56km. The nearest section to EcoBooley is starting at The Vee, six kilometres south of Clogheen, finishing in Ardfinnan, a total of 11.5km. Look out for the old stone hut at the Vee Gap. This was used as a stopping point for sweating horses while passengers alighted from their carriages and took in the mountain air. See www.walkireland.ie for details.

the Midlands

The Midlands

Any cynical sorts, who think that being environmentally-friendly is simply a marketing ploy, should visit Trinity Island. A lakeland retreat on its own forested island, this place is never short of bookings. It is a fishing haven, seconds' walk from the shores of Lough Oughter, where there are boats you could almost fall out of your bed into in the morning. After a day's fishing, you can come back to the wood-heated sauna or jacuzzi bath, and tuck up in front of the fire in the upstairs open-plan kitchen, dining room and lounge. This room reveals the stones of the original barn, contrasting with the wooden beams and floorboards.

t: +353 (0) 49 4334314
w: www.trinityisland.com

The decked terrace overlooks not only Lough Oughter, but also the ruins of the earliest inhabitants here, monks from the Order of Premontre. This Abbey dates back to 1237 and Tom, the generous, welcoming and fun-loving owner of Trinity Island, has worked hard to prevent its total collapse. When I closed the farm gate behind me, and drove the few kilometres down the laneway, past 150 acres of forest, I knew that I was following a road to nowhere. I could see instantly why the monks chose it.

The majority of visitors are fishermen, but as Tom's passion for eco-awareness grows, so does his desire to start sharing it with visitors who are interested in the other aspects of the ecosystem. Not just fish. The Lodge has a windmill and solar panels to generate electricity, and Tom has replanted 200 acres with indigenous broadleaf Oaks, Ash and Larch. We took the two-mile walk around the Island, whispering past badger sets, inhaling the glories of wild garlic, studied the various fungi growing on the lakeshore, and listened to the Teale and Widgeon out on the lake. Tom took us in his Canadian canoe, available free of charge. This is typical of Tom's generous spirit, which comes from a genuine love of this place, his home. That is why he strives to protect it. He grew up on the nearby farm, and the family has lived here for four generations. So there is no way he is going to let it be spoiled for the next ones to come. Friars and fishermen move over, it is time to share this hideaway with the rest of us.

Contact details
Address: Trinity Island Lodge, Killeshandra, County Cavan
Telephone: +353 (0) 49 4334314

Website: www.trinityisland.com
Price: Weekends from €700, weekly rental between €1,100 and €1,400
Opening times: All year round
Disabled access: No disabled access

Getting there slowly
There is a bus to Killeshandra, but only once a week. Take a bus to Cavan (hourly) and taxi 20km to Killeshandra. Tom will meet you to take you to the Island.

Go shopping by canoe
Do your shopping in the nearby town of Killeshandra by canoe. Lough Oughter joins up with the Cullies River, which takes a five-kilometre route into Killeshandra. You can also go further afield to Belturbet, taking the longer five hour canoe trip, with picnic stop-off at Lough Oughter castle. Tom, host extraordinaire, generously offers to collect visitors there after a hard day's canoeing. He throws the canoe in the trailer, and just to make sure you are warmed up, he'll suggest a quick diversion to the Seven Horseshoes pub for Irish coffees.

Eat at O'Dowds
This is a real diner, Irish style, with home-cooked Irish stew, apple pies and a great favourite with locals. Run by Tom's daughter, you can see that the O'Dowds have good hospitality in the genes.
Address: O'Dowds, Main Street, Killeshandra
Telephone: +353 (0) 49 4364840

Two features made this stunning restoration of a 1930's Cavan schoolhouse stand out for my children. The bright red Smeg fridge, taking centre stage in the open-plan ground floor area, and the Wii. The latter was most definitely a first on the green circuit of Ireland. As was the designer wood-burning stove, set flush into a recycled marble chimney, the oak staircase with glass and brushed steel banisters and the recycled rubber roof tiles.

The Old Schoolhouse does, in fact, feel very new. It is a spacious and cleverly designed self-catering property that feels like it's made for sharing. There are four double bedrooms, three with ensuite bathrooms. More signs that Michael McCann, the owner of The Old Schoolhouse, likes to party are the five-burner twin oven cooker, surround sound in the living room, extra long dining table, and two cosy couch areas for collapsing in afterwards. Teenagers in one corner, and cronies by the fire, perhaps. Somehow, the grown-ups always seemed to be the first ones to the pool table though.

However, the gadget-loving owner is also an engineer, who rebuilt the house to his own eco-specifications, installing solar panels, wood pellet boiler, loads of Velux windows to provide passive solar heating, rainwater harvesting system and reed bed. But it's not all boys' toys for Michael, who kindly took us on a tour of one of the best kept secrets in Ireland. The Cavan Burren. Situated in

t: +353 (0) 86 254 8901
w: www.theoldschoolhousecavan.com

the townland of Burren, approximately 10km from the house, this is a mountainous limestone area similar to the famous Burren in County Clare. In the 1950s the area was planted with conifer forest, which resulted in many of the ancient monuments, such as megalithic tombs, huts, and rock art, being preserved. Many are only now being rediscovered, and there is an excellent megalithic trail highlighting them around the forest. There are four bikes at the house, if you want to cycle there.

Back to base, the gadgets were back on, music blaring, and the party began for another night. My boys were in heaven here, and it is still top of the eco-cool list for them. Especially my youngest, age five, who summed it up perfectly; "how come all schools can't be like this, Mum?" It's just too cool for school.

Contact details

Address: The Old Schoolhouse, Meenaslieve, Dowra, County Cavan
Telephone: +353 (0) 86 254 8901
Website: www.theoldschoolhousecavan.com
Price: €600 to €900 per week, depending on season
Opening times: All year round
Disabled access: Good access. One of the ensuite bedrooms is on the ground floor, and designed to suit wheelchair users

Getting there slowly

There is a very infrequent bus service from Drumshanbo to Dowra. From there it is a 6km taxi journey or walk to the Old Schoolhouse. You can also get a bus from Sligo or Enniskillen to Blacklion, which is 21km from Meenaslieve.

Visit the Arigna Mines

The Mines in Arigna are about 30km from The Old Schoolhouse. There has been mining in this area since the Middle Ages, finally finishing in 1990, when the mine closed. Ex-miners give tours of the coalface, where the coal abstraction methods are demonstrated. If you don't want to don a hard hat and go underground, you can stick to the overground exhibition.

Address: Arigna Mines, Arigna, County Roscommon
Telephone: +353 (0) 71 964 6466
Website: www.arignaminingexperience.ie

Eat at Macnean House and Restaurant

There are two conditions to eat at Macnean House. Book a taxi home (12km) as the wine list is irresistible, and book a table well in advance, as this restaurant has won just about every foodie award going. Owner and chef, Neven Maguire, is a major player in promoting sustainability and traceability in food production.

Address: MacNean House & Restaurant, Blacklion, County Cavan
Telephone: +353 (0) 719 853022

Welcome to the Midlands which, for many visitors, is a place to stop over en route to somewhere else. Until I discovered Wineport Lodge. This luxury cedar-clad boutique hotel is a heavenly port of pampering, where each of the 29 rooms, all named after a wine or spirit, look out onto the shores of Lough Ree. As I settled into my room, poured a glass of chilled, and complimentary, Cabernet, I knew instantly that one night was not going to be enough.

There was a storm the night of my stay, but in better weather and, if you are lucky enough to have one, you can come here by boat, following the Shannon-Erne waterway system, and mooring up alongside the Taittinger Lounge. This is where I nestled for most of the evening, tucked up on a huge comfy sofa, forgetting about the elements as a huge wood-burning designer stove kept me toasty warm. Which is impressive, considering this is the only source of heating in the room, and one of the first steps Wineport's owner has taken to cut down on energy usage. But I don't think visitors come here for the environmental policy or to learn about their wastewater wetland system. Romance upstages the reedbeds in this idyllic setting, with a roof terrace hot tub or, if you want more privacy, choose something 'relaxing' or 'refreshing' from the bath menu to be brought to your room. Verbena for waking you up, and lavender for slowing things down, apparently. If this all sounds tacky, it is actually far from it. Wineport Lodge manages to encapsulate fine Irish hospitality, without any sense of elitism or commercialism.

It is not only the bath menu which is impressive. Chef Feargal O'Donnell is a member of Euro-Toques, an organisation which stipulates a culinary code of honour, whereby members promote the culinary traditions of their par-

t: +353 (0) 64 39010
w: www.wineport.ie

ticular region and country. He has created a menu brimming with ingredients sourced through local artisans and, where possible, organic. I sampled the delicate Carpaccio of Wild Salmon with home-baked sourdough for a late supper. The breakfast (in bed) was supreme; buttermilk pancakes topped with layers of pancetta and maple syrup, fresh smoothie and great coffee. Imagine my devastation when another storm meant I had to cut short a morning walk across the local Glasson bog, (details of local walks available at reception). A hot tub, hot stone massage, and hot whisky became my own personal revival menu. Just as well they drive you to the station when you are ready to hit the road. Not that you will want to.

Contact details

Address: Wineport Lodge, Glasson, Athlone, County Westmeath
Telephone: +353 (0) 64 39010
Website: www.wineport.ie
Price: €195-250 per night per room, including breakfast (Saturday night stays incur a supplementary charge). Weekend and mid-week packages available
Opening times: All year round
Disabled access: Excellent facilities. Ground floor is ramped throughout the building, and two ground floor bedrooms are designed to cater for visitors with wheelchairs

Getting there slowly:

Train to Athlone and cycle to Wineport, or they will drive visitors to and from the Glasson village to the station, only a couple of kilometres away.

Visit Clonmacnoise

This place isn't called Wineport for nothing. In the sixth century, local monks imported wine across the sea from France, and ferried it here by boat down the River Shannon from Limerick. Remains of one of the most famous of these monastic settlements can be seen at Clonmacnoise, with ruins of a cathedral, seven churches, two round towers, three high crosses, and the largest collection of early Christian graveslabs in Western Europe.
Address: Clonmacnoise, Shannonbridge, Athlone, County Offaly
Telephone: +353 (0) 90 967 4195

the East

The East

Louth

10

Meath

11

Dublin

09

Wicklow

When architects Delphine and Philip Geoghegan got a chance to work on their own project, they grabbed it. Mercifully, for the community of Ballymurrin, the buildings they chose were the 17th Century Quaker meeting house and out-houses, a fascinating and important part of rural Wicklow's heritage. But this is no coincidence, as sustaining cultural heritage is top of the priority list for these gifted architects. Alongside their family cottage, originally the main meeting house, they have restored the stone milking parlour, and created a stylish fusion of old and new architecture, the like of which I usually drool over in lifestyle magazines. "This was my chance to show people that sustainability is not all about calico and spinach", said Delphine.

Bar the cows, the Geoghegans have worked scrupulously to maintain as many of the original features as possible. The four elegant wood and glass doors which open onto the daffodil-filled rear garden fill each of the original cattle entrances. Resisting any temptation to chop the Parlour into separate buildings, they have preserved the original partitions, which provide a semi-open plan aes-thetic, with one room merging smoothly into another.

The under-floor geothermal heating creates an almost 'soft' warm air, topped up by the roaring designer stove, with a flue which stretches up through the pitched timber rafters. As well as this, the energy from solar panels provides the

majority of the hot water. The Parlour is minimally furnished with pale wood,

t: +353 (0) 40 448 206
w: www.ballymurrin.ie

allowing designer splashes of red or lime green to contrast perfectly with the original dry-stone wall, now painted white with organic paints and lime. Funky designer touches are plentiful, from the resplendent shower heads, and remote-control Velux windows (and blinds) to the coloured halogen lights illuminating the porcelain-tiled corridor which links every carefully planned space.

The Quakers would be proud of the Geoghegans. Not only have they preserved these precious historic buildings, but their hospitality is equal to none, as if they have also inherited the spirit of kindness and integrity for which the Quakers are so famous.

Contact details
Address: The Old Milking Parlour, Ballymurrin House, Kilbride, Wicklow, County Wicklow
Telephone: +353 (0) 40 448 206
Website: www.ballymurrin.ie
Price: From €400 for a low season weekend to €1,100 for a week in peak season
Opening times: All year round

Disabled access: The cottage doesn't have full wheelchair access, as it is built on four different levels, with one or two steps up to each. However, the charming guest annex, right beside the Old Milking Parlour, is available for separate rental. It is on ground level, with ensuite wheelchair-friendly bathroom, and designed with similar old and new concepts

Getting there slowly:
Take the Wicklow bus from Dublin, and get off at The Beehive pub. Otherwise take the train to Wicklow town, and cycle or taxi six kilometres to the house.

Visit the Dominican Convent

Wicklow Town is a hub of good restaurants and pubs, but my favourite spot was the Dominican Convent, just beside the Wicklow Gaol (also worth a visit). It is a must for organic meat and vegetables, all farmed by the nuns. They also have a wide selection of eco-friendly cleaning products, wholefoods, jams and dried fruits. They offer a series of courses and workshops in cookery, gardening and spirituality, as well as free open days of their gardens and farm, overlooking Wicklow Bay, on the first Saturday of every month March-October, starting 11am. Look out for their stall at Farmers' Markets, in Dalkey on Fridays, and Wicklow and Bray, every Saturday.
Address: An Tairseach, Dominican Farm and Ecology Centre, Wicklow Town, County Wicklow
Telephone: +353 (0) 40 461 833
Website: www.ecocentrewicklow.ie

Visit Mount Usher Gardens

On the banks of the River Vartry, Mount Usher has been designed in the style of celebrated 19th Century garden designer, William Robinson. Equally luscious are the shops and café, most of which are run by Avoca, Ireland's leading provider of gourmet foods, local crafts and designer giftware. This is dangerously delicious credit card territory, as you stock up on everything from funky wellies to takeaway treats. Or just plant yourself in the garden café and gorge on all things Avoca.
Address: Ashford, County Wicklow
Telephone: +353 (0) 404 40205
Website: www.mountushergardens.ie

Bellinter House is located only five kilometres from the Hill of Tara which, tradition has it, was the seat of the ancient Kings of Ireland. If ever there was an Irish King of restoration, Jay Bourke should be crowned. His recently restored early 18th Century Palladian house is a coup of restoration and conservation.

The previous owners of this huge elegant mansion were nuns and there is still a hint of modest, sparse design at Bellinter, to the point of being almost functional. But this, for Bourke, was all about conservation. You don't need to add much when you have original features like a giant Bacchae mask carved into the plasterwork in the entrance hall. You don't need to wallpaper the walls if you have original wooden panelling in the vast high-ceilinged bedrooms. Nor do you need to put carpets on all of the original pitch pine floorboards. Strip it back to the bear bones and show it off; that is Jay's philosophy. His biggest bugbear is waste. Just about every piece of furniture here is recycled, refurbished, rebuilt, reupholstered and utterly resplendent. Old velour sofas perch on restored pitch pine floorboards. An ancient pool table is lit by suspended lights, the shades made out of silver salvers. It is felicitous and funky, and yet sparse and practical.

t: +353 (0) 46 903 0900
w: www.bellinterhouse.com

The main house has six bedrooms. All are different, but with similar traits. One of these is the huge cow hide rugs on the floors. "Those are Meath cows, you know", said Jay. This is taking local sourcing to a new level, but if he can keep it local, he will. The lime plastering throughout the buildings was the work of a genius local artisan. The elm tables in the vaulted basement dining room, once the chapel, were handmade by a local carpenter, as were the ash staircases in the Bath House. Each roof slate was diligently replaced by a local period roof expert, and the solid cedar doors were created locally too.

However, the local builders must have thought Jay was mad, when he dug one metre down into a rockery and flowerbed, to reveal the stones from a ruined dairy house, and then asked them to use every single one to restore the building, now the Bath House. This is the only hotel in Ireland where you can have genuine seaweed baths, with sustainably harvested seaweed brought down from Sligo.

The swimming pool is in "an ugly old prefab put up by the Nuns", said Jay, "they all wanted me to pull it down. But that's a waste, so we covered it with zinc, added cedar doors, and it looks great". Which it does. Both this and the outdoor pool will be heated geothermally by the summer, as pipes were already being laid for this during my stay here. Bellinter also has strict recycling policies, and is totally committed to local food sourcing. All water is sourced from their own wells, they have built their own waste water treatment plant, and use environmentally-friendly cleaning products.

We spent the night in the family room in the stables which, like the bathhouse, were rebuilt from ruins. Lime plaster and distressed beams, cedar stable doors and old fused with new furnishings, make this the perfect glamorous and spacious family hideout. Many of the state-of-the-art electrical gadgets are on standby, which is a shame, and heating is from a gas boiler, so it's not eco-perfect. However, in terms of restoring and respecting a precious piece of Irish architectural history, contemporising without compromising, this is inspired. As one guest wrote in the visitor's book, "Oh, what a night". Ours was so good, we stayed for one more.

Contact details
Address: Bellinter House, Navan, County Meath
Telephone: +353 (0) 46 903 0900
Website: www.bellinterhouse.com
Price: €300-360 per room, bed and breakfast, Stables family room, €250-320 per room bed and breakfast
Opening times: Closed 25 and 26 December
Disabled access: One of the stable rooms has been designed for wheelchair access, and there are exterior lifts in the main house and bath house

Getting there slowly
Take the bus from Dublin to Navan, which is a forty-minute journey, and stops nearby to Bellinter House. The staff can collect guests from the bus stop.

Cycle to the Hill of Tara
Borrow one of Bellinter's bikes, and cycle to the Hill of Tara, or continue the ecclesiastical theme and visit Dalgan Park, home to the Irish Missionary Union. The award-winning Mission Awareness Centre archives through photos and film, the people and cultures encountered by Columban missionaries in Asia, the South Pacific and South America. There are also six kilometres of woodland and riverbank walks along the Boyne. See www.imudalganpark.com.

Cultivate is a "Living and Learning Centre" and, I must admit, names like this always put me off a little. I am not sure about the name Cultivate either, really, maybe it is because they all sound like commands, and almost make you feel guilty if you don't live and learn, and cultivate, all at the same time. However, I am sure this was not the intention of the Sustainable Ireland Cooperative which created it.

For me, however, Cultivate is first and foremost a wonderful place in the middle of Dublin, where you can buy all the eco-products you need. They have a great range of cleaning products, stationery, gardening products (as well as a garden centre in the courtyard at the back of the building), and cosmetics. Most interesting to me was their stock of books and magazines on eco-issues, most notably Sustainability, Ireland's only magazine with detailed features on all aspects of sustainability. I also loved the range of Irish products on display, such as the Alagaran seaweed-based cosmetic range, made in Donegal. Or the paper lunchbags made by Lón an Ler in Tipperary. Perfect for picnic lunches if you are heading off to the countryside. I bought a few packets of Irish seeds to send to a friend instead of a postcard, ingeniously produced by www.brownenvelope-seeds.com, and grown on their farm in Skibbereen, West Cork.

Cultivate also runs courses and workshops from the Centre, and is very active in developing a sustainable network throughout Ireland. These include gar-

t: +353 (0) 1 674 5773
w: www.cultivate.ie

dening workshops in the courtyard, bike maintenance one-day classes, Ayurveda Natural Health Seminars and Seaweed workshops. Cultivate is a member of "Stop Climate Chaos", a coalition group of various Irish organisations, which is campaigning to put a stop to Ireland's pollution record, "the sixth most polluting country in the industrialised world.". Their campaign leaflet shows that Ireland emits more climate-changing pollution per person than China, India and Sweden put together. I live and learn.

Contact details
Address: Cultivate, 15-19 Essex St West, Temple Bar, Dublin 8
Telephone: +353 (0) 1 674 5773
Website: www.cultivate.ie
Opening times: Monday-Saturday, 10am-5.30pm
Disabled access: There is wheelchair access to the shop and garden, and lift to workshop area, but bathrooms still need to be converted to assist wheelchair users

Getting there slowly
Take the bus to Dublin city centre. Walk down the boardwalk on the North side of the River Liffey, and cross over Capel Street Bridge towards Cultivate.

Eat at Smock Alley Café
A few doors down from Cultivate, Smock Alley Café serves Organic fairtrade Coffee, and does a wonderful lunchtime deal of soup, savoury tart and tea or coffee for €9. All organic. They often have exhibitions of local artists' work as well. Open 7am until 6pm.
Address: Smock Alley Café, 3-4 Smock Alley Court, West Essex Street, Dublin 8
Telephone: +353 (0) 87 648 5390

the North West

The North West

Greenbox is an organisation which does exactly what it says on the tin. It is a green box of ecotourism in the North West of Ireland, within which visitors can access responsible tourism businesses. These are varied, but generally defined as "small scale, low impact, culturally sensitive, community-orientated and primarily nature-based". It is a cross-border organisation, set up in 2002 and based in Manorhamilton, County Leitrim. It was set up in this region for several reasons. Firstly, Ireland doesn't get much more beautiful than in the North West. Secondly, tourists don't often venture into many of these remote areas and, thirdly, many families in this region are in need of rural diversification in order to survive. Finally, the border areas of this region were once the centre of violence and conflict. Greenbox strives to play its role in the peace and reconciliation process, not only by bringing northern and southern tourism businesses together, but also by encouraging cross-border tourism.

Although it plays a vital role in marketing small sustainable businesses, Greenbox also offers them training, so that they can work towards achieving the green accreditation and European Ecolabel, the EU Flower. This involves reducing energy consumption, water consumption, waste production, favouring the use of renewable resources eco-friendly products, as well as promoting this to their visitors in a positive manner. So now, farmers, yoga teachers, canoeists, restaurant owners and cheese-makers, to name but a few, in the counties of

t: +353 (0) 71 985 6898
w: www.greenbox.ie

Fermanagh, Leitrim, West Cavan, North Sligo, South Donegal and North West Monaghan, can work not only to protect the countryside they are selling, but also ensure that the financial benefits stay in these areas.

Several of our featured ecoescapes are Greenbox members, but it is still extremely worthwhile checking Greenbox's website, as it is an invaluable source of information to any tourists in this region. Greenbox is made up of a small team of committed experts in ecotourism, and always welcomes questions and suggestions. It is growing all the time, and was recently nominated for a Virgin Responsible Tourism Award, as well as becoming a finalist in the Best Destination category of World Travel and Tourism's 'Tourism for Tomorrow' Awards 2007. The other two finalists were The State of Vermont and The Great Barrier Reef. This international recognition has led to the continued growth of the Greenbox, whose list of members grows all the time.

One of the Greenbox's most impressive achievements is the creation of the 'Greenbox Ecotourism Package', which encourages everyone from bed and breakfast owners to film-makers to create an interesting and sustainable 'package' for visitors. Creative tourism entrepreneurs include a Donegal language school which teaches English in the morning and surfing in the afternoon, wildlife film-making courses in Enniskillen, and the Wilderness Therapy weekends on Lough Allen.

Greenbox is unstoppable, and many tourist boards are now looking to them for inspiration, to understand ways in which they too can achieve such dynamic changes in attitude in their region. Let's hope that by opening the lid on this exemplary box, the effect will be a positive and nationwide one.

Contact details
Address: Greenbox, Park Rd Industrial Estate, Manorhamilton, County Leitrim
Telephone: +353 (0) 71 985 6898
Website: www.greenbox.ie

This looped cycle trail is the best slap in the face for those who grumble that Ireland is now a concrete jungle full of alien architecture and Audis. Forests, lakes and farms are just about all you see on the 370 kilometres of carefully sign-posted and mapped trail around five counties of the North West.

The Kingfisher is an appropriate name for Ireland's first long-distance cycle trail. It is associated with lakelands, and as this Trail twists in and out of the extraordinarily endless lakes of Cavan, Fermanagh, Leitrim and Monaghan, the Kingfisher has superb choices of shores to rest upon. Visitors who are new to these counties will be knocked out by the vast network of waterways feeding off, among others, the River Erne which, in turn, steers its way down a natural corridor to Donegal Bay. The trail was started as a cross-border initiative in 1995 and, at certain points along the way, it is hard to know if you are in the North or the South, so keep a selection of currencies to hand. Consequently, it is co-marketed by the British cycling charity Sustrans and Greenbox, and maintained by the relevant local authorities.

The figure of eight route is divided into two loops. The northern loop circles the whole of Lower Lough Erne, alongside Loughs Melvin and Macnean, stretching out as far as Ballyshannon in County Donegal. The lower loop is bordered on two sides by Upper Lough Erne and Lough Allen. A good starting point for the southern loop is Carrick-on-Shannon, from where you can travel east, along back-

t: +353 (0) 71 98 56898
w: www.cycletoursireland.com

roads through the patchwork quilt-like landscape of tiny lakes. On this route, an ideal picnic stop is at Newtownbutler where, If travelling anti-clockwise, you have to phone the ferryman to help you back on your journey across the lake to Crom. For the northern loop section, hire bikes at Corralea Activity Centre (see page 116), and base yourself here for a few days. Then go further north, and check out the extra Atlantic mini-loop from Belleek or Ballyshannon to the sandy beach at Rossnowlagh. Creevy Cottages is the perfect stop-off for this part of the loop.

The map to the Kingfisher is excellent, offering several different ways to break up the Trail, as well as day routes and tourist attractions along the way. It also points out some of the busier sections of road, warning cyclists to take caution, but there are few of these.

Many of our ecoescapes are dotted along or near The Kingfisher Trail. These include The Old Schoolhouse, Orchard Acre Farm, Corralea Activity Centre, Little Crom Cottages, Creevy Cottages, The Breesy Centre, Lough Allen Adventure Centre, The Old Rectory, Trinity Island Lodge, The Share Holiday Village, Blaney Spa and Yoga Centre and Ard na Breatha. So it is possible to cycle your way around the whole trail and support sustainable businesses en route. Most of them will arrange bike hire, or have bikes available for use. Good off-road cycling for children can be found on the sections at Crom Estate, Castle Archdale and Florence Court, all in County Fermanagh.

The closest train railway stations near or on the Trail are Sligo and Carrick-on-Shannon, although Bus Eireann and Ulsterbus are both happy to carry bicycles if there is room in the luggage section of the coach.

Contact details

For more information and maps of the Trail contact:

Address: The Kingfisher Cycle Trail, C/O The Green Box, Park Rd Industrial Estate, Manorhamilton, County Leitrim

Website: www.cycletoursireland.com

or

Address: Sustrans, Marquis Building, 89-91 Adelaide Street, Belfast BT2 8FE

Telephone: +44 (0) 28 9043 4569

Website: www.sustrans.org.uk

Benwiskin, the main peak of the Dartry Mountains, is central to everything here. It rises out of the earth like a giant tipi, overlooking the equally magnificent Benbulben. This is the dramatic backdrop for this small community-run hostel in Ballintrillick village. It was set up originally by the local environmental group, to combat illegal dumping on their otherwise perfect landscape. They have now refurbished this old schoolhouse, and succeeded in bringing it up to good eco-friendly standards, by installing a wood pellet boiler and solar panels, which provide heating and hot water. There are so many notices about recycling and energy-saving, I was afraid to put a foot wrong.

This building is a credit to the community. It continues to employ four local full-time staff and all profits are ploughed back into the building. It not only serves as a hostel, but as a community centrepoint, with classes and workshops through-out the winter. They have a detailed list of cycle and walking routes (with four bikes to hire at the hostel), and during my brief stay I embarked on two of these. One was a gentle cycle into the lower foothills of Benbulben, which took me close enough to see the countless waterfalls tumbling down the deeply carved gorges. This was a mere warm-up for my next walk, into the Gleniff Horse-

t: +353 (0) 71 917 6721
w: www.benwiskincentre.com

shoe Valley. Twelve kilometres of the most unforgettable walking in Ireland. I was travelling here in March, alone, and had only the sheep to accompany me on the mountain road. As I was walking alone, I felt safe on the road, rather than taking any off-road paths, all of which are strictly by private access only.

I passed the famous cave where, according to Irish myth, lovers Gráinne and Diarmuid, spent their last night together before dying, watched on and unaided by jilted lover Fionn. I stood looking across this vast cavern, the gently falling snow highlighting every crevice and valley of this most remote and rousing Sligo mountainside. If ever there was a landscape made to encapsulate myths and magic, this must surely be it.

Contact details

Address: Benwiskin Centre, Ballintrillick, County Sligo
Telephone: +353 (0) 71 917 6721
Website: www.benwiskincentre.com
Price: A bed in a shared dorm costs €15. There is also a room tariff, sleeping four, at €60. The Centre, sleeping 26, can be booked by one group at a price of €350 for the first night and €300 for subsequent nights
Opening times: Open all year round
Disabled access: Good wheelchair access with ramp and rail into Centre

Getting there slowly

Not the easiest, as this is really out of the way, but you can take a bus to Bundoran (with change at Ballyshannon), and then taxi, 11km to Ballintrillick. Buy food before you get there as the nearest shop is five kilometres away from the Centre. The other alternative is to take a bus or train to Sligo, and get a taxi or, if you are up to it, cycle 27 kilometres. Catch Sligo Farmers' Market on a Saturday to stock up. See Farmers' Market section for details on pages 146-147.

Eat at the Coach Lane

It's well worth the trip into Sligo to eat at the Coach Lane restaurant @ Donaghy's bar. With its traditional, welcoming pub downstairs, you can have the best Irish starter of a pint, and then upstairs for a rich menu of gastronomic treats. It all began well, with the mini-loaf of half cheese, half chilli. The rest of the meal just got better and better, and although I went for the 'catch of the day', which was excellent, they have an extensive meat menu, all Bord Bia certified, for traceability. Booking is advisable.

Address: Coach Lane Restaurant @ Donaghy's Bar, 1-2 Lord Edward Street, Sligo, County Sligo
Telephone: +353 (0) 71 916 2417

The Irish have discovered a healing weed, which is legal. Like so many ancient traditions, the use of seaweed baths to aid rheumatism, arthritis or general aches and pains, is being revived. You lock yourself into your own bathroom, or share a room with whoever your idea of a good weed companion is (there are two baths, so it doesn't have to get too intimate). At Voya, all the rolltop baths are recycled, many of them rescued from fields where they were being used as cattle troughs. Now that's good recycling for you.

Then into your steamroom to open up the pores, so that the weed can kick in faster I suppose, and then you have to confront the bucket of seaweed. This is the real thing, picked that morning from the local shore, not some sort of chemically produced powder. It's green and slimy, and I used to run screaming from it as a child. Now they wanted me to bathe in it and enjoy it. I threw my bucketful of seaweed into the bath, pre-filled to the brim with steaming seawater, piped from just across the road, and took the plunge. The seaweed turned instantly from slimy to soft, from 'uugh' to 'oooh'. The last part of the weed ritual is the cold shower. And despite the impressive range of complimentary Voya products available, they do recommend going cold turkey. No products, no comforts. Just a cold shower to close the pores, but making sure all the good oily bits stay on. 'Coming down' from the weed is harsh indeed, but I had a quick last fix of Fuscius and dived in one last time for one last hit.

Voya is a family-run business, with the two sons, Neil and Mark, managing the building and products. Their dad, also an organic vegetable farmer, does the daily harvest of seaweed. They do so sustainably, with a Department of Marine licence to cut the seaweed 50km left and right of Strandhill seafront, where

t: +353 (0) 71 916 8686
w: www.voya.ie

their baths are located. They walk out at low tide, and cut the seaweed growing on the reef, to three quarter length. This then grows back fully within twelve months. The used seaweed (a tonne and a half a week) is then distributed to various organic farms for use as fertiliser.

Afterwards, I felt thoroughly cleansed, exhausted and exhilarated. All muscle ache after a hard day's walking in the Sligo hills was long gone, apparently due to the high concentrations of iodine which eases any aches and pains. At €22 it is also great value. I call that cheap weed, man.

Contact details
Address: Voya Seaweed Baths, Strandhill, County Sligo
Telephone: +353 (0) 71 916 8686
Website: www.voya.ie
Price: Single seaweed bathroom €22, double bathing room €40
Opening times: All year round, 10am-8pm
Disabled access: Good wheelchair access. Handrails on all baths and steam cabinets are on one level. Plans to have mobile hoist in baths by the end of 2009

Getting there slowly
Take the train or bus to Sligo, and the connecting bus to Strandhill, only eight kilometres from Sligo. You can also take the back roads if you want to cycle.

Other seaweed experiences in Ireland
There are three other seaweed bath houses in Ireland, and each has its own ways of doing things. All four bathhouses offer a selection of treatments to accompany the seaweed baths, from seaweed body wraps to seaweed hot stone massage. Bellinter House (page 55) and Delphi Mountain Resort (page 139) also offer Voya's organic seaweed bath experiences.

Address: Soak Seaweed Baths, 5a South Promenade, Newcastle, County Down BT33 0EX.
Phone: +44 (0) 28 4372 6002
Website: www.soakseaweedbaths.co.uk (more information on page 174)

Address: Kilcullen Seaweed Baths, Enniscrone, County Sligo
Telephone: +353 (0) 96 36238
Website: www.kilcullenseaweedbaths.com (more information on page 172)

Address: Bundoran Water World, Sea Front, Bundoran, County Donegal
Telephone: +353 (0) 71 9841 172
Website: www.waterworldbundoran.com

The Gyreum breaks all the rules. It is round, and its roof, a dark green cone, slopes down to grass roots level, just begging to be climbed over, sunbathed on, stargazed from and smiled upon. The 30 second journey from terrain to tip, with its views over Lough Arrow and rural Sligo, transformed me from forty to four. So did the inside, a bit like a giant yurt with bedrooms and bathrooms slotted into its stone walls, giving them a cave-like cosiness.

Everything is recycled here. More precisely, nothing is new. The curtains look like they were 'run up' by Colum, the creator of this bit of malevolent madness, and the furniture has a 'late night run around the skips' feel about it. You either love it or hate it, and I'll stick with the loving group. I loved its mustiness, I loved the living centre of the building with its geothermally heated flagstone floor, and I loved the fireplace. This vast wood-burning stove is the Gyreum's centrepiece, the epicentre where visitors hang out on battered armchairs, taking turns to stoke the fire, as if passing the talking stick.

The Gyreum is an antidote to crisp, cold, tourism 'commodities'. As well as traditional toilets, connected to a reed bed, there is an outside compost loo. The baths, old rolltops which have seen better days, are quirky rather than dirty. The step ladder up to the crow's nest library room is not for vertigo sufferers or young children. All these features make the Gyreum worth celebrating. That and its eco-awareness, with a windmill and solar panels to be added to the list.

t: +353 (0) 71 91 65994
w: www.gyreum.com

During my winter visit, there were ten tents erected inside as they had so many visitors. If that doesn't make you smile, don't even think of staying here. If it does, then seek out this place which looks like it grew out of the Sligo hills just to break the tourist mould in the most imaginative and earthy way possible.

Contact details
Address: The Gyreum, Corlisheen, Riverstown, County Sligo
Telephone: +353 (0) 71 91 65994
Website: www.gyreum.com
Price: €17-27 per person
Opening times: All year
Disabled access: There is a ramp to the main entrance. One dorm and bathroom are wheelchair accessible but there are steps down to the self-catering kitchen area

Getting there slowly
Take the train to Sligo, Ballymote or Collooney, then taxi to Riverstown. Gyreum will arrange bike hire for visitors.

Take the Pilgrim's Progress Tour
Run by The Gyreum, this is a seven-day 250km circuit on land, sea and lake, covering six counties of Ireland, starting and ending at The Gyreum. Visiting Celtic Hermits' dens, monastic sites on remote islands, sweat lodges and ending with a 24 hour retreat in time for the full moon. See website for details of monthly tours.

Eat at Clevery Mill
In Castlebaldwin, Clevery Mill is where head chef Diarmuid grows much of the grub himself. This is a forty-five minute walk from The Gyreum or a fifteen minute cycle. The menu changes regularly and includes fillet of Riverstown beef with smoked bacon galette potatoes as well as other locally reared meat.
Address: Clevery Mill, Castlebaldwin, County Sligo
Telephone: +353 (0) 71 912 7424
Website: www.cleverymill.com

Hundreds of wild deer roam freely throughout the O'Hara's vast estate at Coopershill, and so it is with some amusement that the young owner, Simon, stuck his hat on the antlers, now the family hatstand which takes pride of place in the centre of the grand entrance hall. Second only to the vast wood-burning stove, heating the entire 18th Century granite mansion, and which warmed me up the minute I came in from the cold.

Simon belongs to the seventh generation of O'Haras to live at Coopershill since it was built in 1774. He is committed to all the principles of grand hospitality, Irish style. And sustainability, with its working farm, rainwater harvesting system, natural spring water, and wetlands sewage system. There are eight elegant ensuite rooms, all with traditional décor, maintaining as much of the original furnishings as possible. Grandfather clocks, four poster beds, and floor to ceiling gilded mirrors. One of the most striking features is a Victorian roll-top bath, with original fully-integrated cast-iron shower. There was a party going on the weekend I visited, and a general sense of fun and friendship around the place. Coopershill, although grand and elegant, does not take itself too seriously. There is a snooker room in the basement, hats on antlers, and smiling O'Haras at every return of the spiral staircase. It's as if the house has absorbed the warmth of seven generations of welcoming souls.

t: +353 (0) 71 916 5108
w: www.coopershill.com

The recent development of deer farming has involved a lot of work, and yet it is the most fitting form of rural diversification. We visited during the winter, when the deer are brought inside to let the pasture develop. Simon gave my kids a tour of the deer stalls, letting us have a distant peak at the timid creatures feeding. As my children delighted in the Bambiness of it all, I, the hardened carnivore of a mother, delighted in the family speciality of pot roast venison. Slow food is part of the ethos at Coopershill, with a family-run sheep farm on the adjoining property, and many of the fruit and vegetables served from the kitchen gardens. All eaten off family silver, which is fitting, because when you stay at Coopershill, that is just how you are made to feel. Like one of the family.

Contact details
Address: Coopershill House, Riverstown, County Sligo
Telephone: +353 (0) 71 916 5108
Website: www.coopershill.com
Price: From €109-136, per person per night including breakfast
Opening times: 1 April until the end of October, although the house is open for house parties during the 'closed' season
Disabled access: None

Getting there slowly
Take the train to Sligo, Ballymote or Collooney, then taxi to Riverstown. Even better, why not send your luggage in a taxi, and you can do the rest by bike.

Visit the Sligo Folk Park
The Sligo Folk Park is a tiny museum in Riverstown, just a quick walk from Coopershill House. The Folk Park is a community-run attraction and provides a glimpse of 19th Century rural and Irish heritage. There is a wonderful museum and exhibition hall where visitors can see one of Ireland's finest collections of agricultural artefacts. There is a pretty fine collection of locally-made cakes on sale in the café too.
Address: Sligo Folk Park, Millview House, Riverstown, County Sligo
Telephone: +353 (0) 71 916 5001
Website: www.sligofolkpark.com

There are many reasons for travelling to this hostel out of season, but I am not sure that getting to learn the 'slush dance' was one of them. When you choose to stay at a rural community centre in mid-January, this is the sort of cultural delight in store for you. And it truly was a delight. With activities for the local community throughout the autumn and winter, such as barn dance classes (I had the honour of dancing with every Cashelard man in one night), yoga classes and concerts, you are more than welcome to join in, if you are spending a night here.

Visit in the 'right season', however, and you can learn more than a quick step. Come March, things step up a pace. Activity weekend breaks include hill walking, surfing, horseriding, kayaking and fishing. With 22 lakes within a 8km radius, and two prize beaches at Rossnowlagh and Murvagh, they are not short of locations. Walk out the main door and straight up the hill behind the Centre, following the reeds along the banks of Lough Colmcille, and you come to Breesy Hill. The reward of a half hour climb is views over the lakes, lowlands and highlands of six counties. A further hour's walk around the lake brought me back to Breesy, where I nursed my waltz-and walking-weary muscles in the comfort of the self-catering kitchen. They kindly lay out an all-day breakfast, and I helped myself to cereal, yoghurt, fresh fruit and coffee.

t: +353 (0) 71 982 2925
w: www.breesycentre.com

The Breesy Centre runs a tight ship in terms of environmentally-friendly

practices. They have a strict recycling system, composting, energy restrictions, and energy-saving lightbulbs. Its new extension, opening July 2008, provides two additional bedrooms, and a small self-catering apartment. It has geo-thermal heating and solar panels, aimed at heating 90 per cent of the building's hot water. The community centre has had a huge impact here. Until ten years ago, the population was diminishing quickly, and Breesy has played a hugely significant role in stopping the rapid depopulation of this rural Donegal townland. Maybe it's all that dancing.

Contact details
Address: The Breesy Centre, Cashelard, Ballyshannon, County Donegal
Telephone: +353 (0) 71 982 2925
Website: www.breesycentre.com
Price: €32 per person per night bed & Continental breakfast, €38 per person per night Bed and Full Irish breakfast
Opening times: All year round
Disabled access: One of the ground-floor bedrooms, and the new self-catering apartment, are designed to assist wheelchair users

Getting there slowly
Take a bus to Ballyshannon, and a taxi to the Centre. Otherwise it's a five kilometre cycle.

Drink at the Travellers' Rest
Conveniently across the road from the Centre, the Travellers' Rest is famous for being the first place where Tony Blair drank Guinness. His grandfather was a Cashelard man, and his mother was born in Ballyshannon.

Eat at Shannon's Corner
Shannon's Corner specialises in home-made roasts, all supplied from local farms. "I can tell you the herd number of every bit of beef I buy", Mary, the owner and chef told me. There are plenty of walks around to work off her superb home made traditional desserts such as pavlova or apple pie. Opens from 8am-5pm. The home-made scones for breakfast are also recommended.
Address: Shannon's Corner, Bishop Street, Ballyshannon, County Donegal
Telephone: +353 (0) 71 98 51180

I passed a new housing estate and a dual carriageway to get to this gorgeous guesthouse in the Donegal hills. Needless to say, I had my worries. But not as many as Theresa and Albert Morrow, the farmers who own this most unlikely eco-spot, have had. "I accept that this is progress. I used to have to go into town, and now they are bringing the town out to me", said Theresa with her big grin and 'not a bother' attitude. It is this attitude which has kept them in business. That and the fact that they are exemplary hosts who make you want to never leave the Donegal hills.

Ard na Breatha is not only a green guesthouse, but also a thriving restaurant specialising in local, seasonal and organic produce. The lamb couldn't be more local. It is from their own farm. The chef couldn't be more local either. It is Albert himself, who recently retrained and may now be the only working farmer cum chef in the country. What makes Ard na Breatha stand out in terms of ecoawareness is the Morrows' determination to 'make a difference'. They signed up for the EU Flower green accreditation scheme because, "Within a year of working in tourism, I realised how much damage we were doing to the environment", said Theresa. They changed to a green electricity supplier, every single lightbulb was replaced, they compost or recycle everything they can and use environmentally-friendly cleaning and visitors' bathroom products. "It has saved us a lot of money. So we are saving up to get a wood pellet boiler and solar panels," Theresa added.

But it is not green policies (or Albert's cuisine) alone which bring visitors to Ard na Breatha. It is the Donegal hills. Take a three-kilometre cycle to Lough Eske, and continue around the Lough for approximately twenty kilometres.

t: +353 (0) 74 972 2288
w: www.ardnabreatha.com

These roads are generally quiet, except on Sundays when drivers go for a carvery lunch at the nearby hotel. Outside this window, you can ride the roads which link up the Bluestack Mountains, breathe in the abundant wet moss and ferns being fed by the River Eske, and finish back in Ard na Breatha for a fine bit of roast lamb.

Contact details
Address: Ard na Breatha,
Drumrooske Middle,
Donegal Town, County Donegal
Telephone: +353 (0) 74 972 2288
Website: www.ardnabreatha.com
Price: From €40-€55 per person
sharing, depending on season. Five
course dinner €42.50
Opening times: Closed November
to January
Disabled access: No wheelchair access

Getting there slowly
Take the bus to Donegal Town. It is a fifteen-minute walk to the guest house, but Theresa or Albert will collect you from the bus station if you have luggage. It is also on the Kingfisher Cycle Route if you want to cycle here, or you can hire bikes through Ard na Breatha, and have them delivered directly to the door.

In 1987 Creevy Pier was destroyed by storms. Soon after, three local fishermen perished because they had no safe berthage. It is times like this that a community pulls together. The Creevy Cooperative was set up to help the local community derive some additional income through tourism. With Rossnowlagh Blue Flag beach on their doorstep and the nearest town being Ballyshannon, world-renowned for salmon fishing, they were right to do so.

What Creevy has created is exemplary, as I found at Kitty's House, one of the traditional cottages they preserved and restored for visitors. The stonework is unmistakeably the work of local craftsmen who know and love their natural resources. Same with the flagstones on the floors. And the huge traditional fireplace, which was roaring to welcome me. All the homes are named after people who once lived there. Kitty has passed on, but with the help of the Creevy Coop, she has left a fine legacy overlooking her now revived pier. Or you could opt for Big Jimmy's House in a more remote spot a couple of kilometres up in the hills, with views of Tullan Strand that haven't changed since Jimmy's day.

t: +353 (0) 71 985 2896
w: www.creevyexperience.com

Creevy Cooperative members have

also created a ten-mile coastal walk, convenient to the cottages. This is maintained by local men, some of whom also care for the cottage gardens. You might meet Tony or David mowing your lawn, but you will not, however, find them killing weeds. At least not with chemicals. This is because Creevy has signed up to the environmental accreditation EU Flower Scheme and is wholly committed to good green practices. They water gardens with conserved rainwater, manage recycled waste, and there are compost bins (made out of recycled wood by some of the Coop members) in all gardens. The lightbulbs are energy-saving, and cleaning products bio-degradeable. I particularly loved the lemon juice and vinegar bottles left for visitors, with a note explaining the anti-bacterial and cleaning properties of both. That's Creevy for you. A community which grew in strength through good common sense. It has paid off, and being part of it was a great experience. Thus the name of their website.

Contact details
Address: Creevy Cooperative, Ballyshannon, County Donegal
Telephone: +353 (0) 71 985 2896
Website: www.creevyexperience.com and www.countrybreaks.ie
Price: €585-899 per week
Opening times: All year round
Disabled access: Wheelchair access to all cottages. In one of the kitchens, the worktops have been adapted for wheelchair users

Getting there slowly

Creevy Coop will arrange to pick up anyone arriving by bus to Ballyshannon, and take you direct to your chosen cottage. It is approximately a 7km cycle from your cottage into Ballyshannon. If you want to hire bikes, Creevy can arrange for them to be delivered to your cottage.

Sail the An Dúanaí Mara

Charter the Creevy Cooperative boat, An Dúanaí Mara for a day. Skippered by one of the local fisherman, you can go sea angling, bird watching, or discover the dramatic Donegal seascapes such as Sliabh League, Europe's highest sea cliffs. Contact Creevy Coop or www.duanaimaracharters.com for details.

Eat at The Creevy Pier Hotel

Eat fresh fish and chips at The Creevy Pier Hotel, not with the same amount of character as Kitty's or Jimmy's on the outside, but full of wonderful Donegal characters on the inside.
Address: Creevy Pier Hotel, Creevy Pier, Ballyshannon, County Donegal
Telephone: +353 (0) 71 985 8356
Website: www.creevypierhotel.com

I thought I had died and gone to eco-heaven. Even the architectural design of the Ard Nahoo site, comprising of treatment rooms, yoga studio, and three self-catering lodges, is described as 'spiritual'. Noeleen, the owner, went through a type of therapy with her architect to visualise and create her ideal sustainable space. No wonder she smiles like an angel when she talks about it. "I feel like I am standing in a dream", she told me. This joy is infectious.

On arrival I found it hard just to leave the comfort of the reception, with its adobe-style clay fireplace. But next step to heaven was our eco-cabin. Made from Donegal cedar, it is cleverly designed to accommodate as many people as possible. The bespoke berth-like beds for children, and the young at heart, are too cute for words. It is insulated with hemp, painted in gentle shades with eco-friendly paints and heated by the most beautiful wood pellet stoves I have ever seen in Ireland. As well as our pre-ordered organic veggie box, Noeleen had left us a welcome pack of local goodies. Together with the honesty shop stocked with organic and eco produce, we realised that we didn't have to move for days. The longest walk was from massage table to steam room to hot tub, overlooking Lough Nahoo.

Noeleen's seven looped trails quickly gave me the will to walk again, and there are also a few bikes for visitors' use. Dromahair village is only a kilometre or two away and worth it for the cheese shop alone. My kids were happy just playing on the acre and a half of rock which protects the lodges from the ele-

t: +353 (o) 71 91 34939
w: www.ardnahoo.com

ments. For those who want kid-free time, opt for a pamper package weekend. If there is a big enough group, they will even collect you from Dublin or Sligo and drive you to their specially-sculpted pearly gates in the local eco-bus, run on vegetable oil. Heaven doesn't get much better than this.

Contact details
Address: Ard Nahoo, Mullagh, Dromahair, County Leitrim
Telephone: +353 (0) 71 91 34939
Website: www.ardnahoo.com
Price: Prices start from €190 per cabin (not including treatments)
Opening times: All year
Disabled access: The new wooden cabins have been built to facilitate wheelchair users

Getting there slowly
Take the train to Sligo and from there it's a twenty minute taxi drive costing approximately €20. For large groups, you can discuss the possibility of collection in the eco-bus.

Visit the Leitrim Sculpture Centre
The Sculpture Centre is in Manorhamilton, a town which is now a veritable artists' hub. It offers studio and gallery space to some of the country's most prolific artists, working in bronze, wood, ceramics and stone. The Centre also runs workshops and masterclasses in everything from glass-blowing to calligraphy in stone.
Website: www.leitrimsculpturecentre.ie

Drink at Stanford's Inn
Drink at Stanford's Inn, but treat yourself to the set menu (one for kids too) at The Riverbank, where the chef is a local man who understands the importance of keeping things local.
Address: Riverbank Restaurant, Dromahair, Co. Leitrim
Telephone: +353 (0) 71 91 64934
Website: www.riverbank-restaurant.com

When I admired Nuala's cool triple recycling bins in the apartment, which is cleverly attached onto her own wooden house, she told me, "I have a triple composting system. First I feed the cat, then I go down the hill to my neighbour's horse, and finally some carrot-ends to his donkey". This is Nuala, who thinks of everything and everyone. The first sign of such kindness was the welcome parcel on the kitchen counter. It was full of local chutneys, jam, herbs, elderflower cordial and fairtrade chocolate. Her willingness to share her local knowledge was equally generous. "That's why I built it. I love to share Leitrim", she told me. Indeed, first thing I wanted to do when I got here was run. Just jump off the wooden veranda, down the hill, into the sodden verdant valley, gathering enough speed to run up the bronze coloured Ballinabehy ridge, and finally cool off in Munakill Lake.

But of course, this only happens in movies, where they don't have farmers and land access problems. But Nuala grew up here, and knows all the welcoming farmers. She even helps run a hill-walking club called Holey Soles, with a special 'holey' Easter walking festival. If you have kids, she will take you all down to her brother's farm in the next field. Catch them in lambing season and you are in for a real treat. Her local knowledge has helped her in setting up a weekend package of nature and archaeology walks. Ask Nuala where to go mushroom foraging, and she'll point you in the right direction.

t: +353 (0) 71 982 0083
w: www.tawnylustlodge.com

Environmentally-friendly too, with solar passive heating, solar panels for

hot water, low wattage under floor heating, recycled paper insulation, an inbuilt heat recovery system, and electricity from a renewable energy company. She keeps things local, with Leitrim artists' work on the walls and information on all local markets and cooperatives. Leitrim County Council uses the rather unimaginative slogan "Lovely Leitrim", on their signposts. I prefer Nuala's "I love to share Leitrim". Better on the ear and an accurate description of many Leitrim people I met on my travels. If I were them, I would be tempted to keep it a secret.

Contact details
Address: Tawnylust Lodge, Tawnylust, Manorhamilton, County Leitrim
Telephone: +353 (0) 71 982 0083
Website: www.tawnylustlodge.com
Price: Weekend walking, archaeology, nature and foraging packages from €150 per person. Self-catering only from €285-355 for weekend and €485-555 for week, depending on the season. The apartment sleeps up to four
Opening times: All year round
Disabled access: Good access with ramp to apartment and wet room shower

Getting there slowly
Take the bus to Manorhamilton and taxi 9km to Tawnylust. Call +353 (0) 86 854 1777 for a taxi or Nuala can pick you up if she is available.

Go to the pictures
Check out Reels on Wheels, an ingenious and charming mobile cinema, in the back of a truck. Every Wednesday beside the firestation in nearby Manorhamil-

ton, and visiting other Leitrim towns during the week. It was Winterbottom on wheels the week I was there. Just when I thought I had seen it all. See www.leitrimcinema.ie for all listings.

Eat at Clancy's of Glenfarne

On the main N16 road, I stopped here for a top breakfast on an early morning trip to the lakes in Enniskillen. If the eight baking bowls on the kitchen table aren't proof enough of the home made bread, the smell will be. Like many Irish restaurants, they subscribe to Bord Bia (The Irish Food Board), ensuring all food products are sourced locally and traceable 'from farm to fork'.

Address: Clancys of Glenfarne, Brockagh, Glenfarne, County Leitrim
Telephone: +353 (0) 71 985 3116
Website: www.clancysofglenfarne.com

This is the Centre for all that is good and green in Ireland. It is a veritable hive of eco-activity situated at the foot of the Rossinver Mountains. Don't just come here for a cup of organic coffee, organise your holiday around it and spend a day, weekend or longer learning one of the many skills offered by the team of thirty eco-devotees. The building itself is organic, having grown to accommodate interest and demand since its beginnings in 1995. It opened its impressive (and locally-sourced) timber building, with a living grass roof, in 2001, and today offers 150 courses and farms nineteen acres of land. The building, with its recycled paper insulation, wood-pellet boiler and passive solar energy, is the hub of the Centre, where you can study, eat, drink and shop.

I was able to see (and taste) the fruits of many students' labour on my tour around the various demonstration gardens. A dry stone spiral displaying over 20 varieties of mint was the creation of students on a dry stone wall building course, the reed bed system is maintained and developed by students and employees, the fetch (a cross between a fence and a hedge), which lines the senses gardens, was the work of the living willow sculpture experts. Not forgetting the extensive polytunnel system, willow field and orchards serving many workshops from organic fruit and vegetable growing to wood energy courses. The Organic Centre also organises open days, such as Potato Day, Garden Party, Apple Day and participate in the annual Harvest Feast (www.harvestfeast.ie) in September.

t: +353 (0) 71 985 4338
w: www.theorganiccentre.ie

One of their dilemmas is getting people here – carbon footprint was not such a big issue when it chose this remote location way back in the last century. However, it is right on the Kingfisher Cycle Trail, so it's perfectly possible to save on carbon by arriving by bicycle. They also strive to link course members up with one another in advance, to see if car shares are feasible. If medals were awarded to green organisations, these guys should be given one in the form of a green bio bus.

Contact details
Address: The Organic Centre, Rossinver, County Leitrim
Telephone: +353 (0) 71 985 4338
Website: www.theorganiccentre.ie
Price: Approximately €90 for one-day courses, and €190 for 2-day course. The 3-day Polytunnel course costs €250
Opening times: The Centre is open all year round from 10am-5pm closing at Christmas and New Year. The Café is open March-September
Disabled access: Excellent wheelchair facilities

Getting there slowly
You can cycle, following the Kingfisher Cycle Trail, or take a bus to Manorhamilton and walk (a beautiful 11 kilometres), or take a taxi.

The Wilderness Therapy Weekend is one of the specials on the menu here at Lough Allen, so when I phoned to ask for directions, Kevin, the owner told me, "The nearest town is Drumshanbo". "Is there a sign?" I asked, "No, we're in the hills, we don't want anyone to find us", he said. I took this to be my first test. Of course, Kevin was teasing, and in fact it is not hard to find the Centre, which hugs the Lough Shore just outside Ballinagleragh. This Centre is not about tests, and nor is the wilderness therapy weekend. The name of it sounds more like a military-style putting you through your paces, than a fun get away. "I just want people to find out what wilderness really means. There isn't much of it left in Ireland and after participating in this weekend, people can go off and discover a bit of wilderness close to home, even if it's at the bottom of their garden."

Kevin devised this weekend escape to the islands of Lough Allen for school groups. It became so popular, that adult groups started to enquire about it. They make rafts by tying canoes together with barrels, shelters out of ponchos, build fires and forage, cook outdoors, sleep in hammocks, and laugh a lot. My memories of outward bound sadistic teachers from my youth were, thankfully, shattered. It is quite the opposite here, and not at all intimidating. In fact, the Centre itself is not exactly a tightly-run ship, with a website that needs updating, and leaflets which need reprinting. But this for all the right reasons, "Because I am out on the water ninety per cent of the time", said the eternally effervescent Kevin, whose love of the outdoors is totally infectious.

t: +353 (0) 71 964 3292
w: www.loughallenadventure.com

However, he underplays his achievements, having just opened his new state-of-the-art Donegal cedarwood building. This is where he leads all his classes, serves meals and has created a general hanging-out area. In the new changing area, there are showers running off solar-generated hot water, which also heats the new buildings, backed up by a wood-burning boiler. At the Centre, you can hire canoes, windsurfers, have swimming lessons or just use it as base for going hiking. However, the best bet is to get a big enough group together, minimum six, and book in for a weekend on the islands. Be even braver and do it in winter. Just don't forget to pack a sense of humour.

Contact details
Address: Lough Allen Adventure Centre, Ballinagleragh, County Leitrim
Telephone: +353 (0) 71 964 3292
Website: www.loughallenadventure.com
Price: Wilderness Therapy weekend €190 per person
Opening times: Closed for two weeks over Christmas period
Disabled access: Excellent wheelchair access to all buildings

Getting there slowly
Take the train to Carrick-on-Shannon and bus to Drumshanbo. Otherwise take the bus to Dowra. The Centre can arrange pick-ups if necessary.

Eat at the Melrose Inn
It is worth the cycle ride (just under 5km) to Dowra to have a pint at the Melrose Inn, locally known as Mel's. This is a very friendly, cosy village pub, where there is always a welcoming fire, bar food and traditional music at weekends.

When I was growing up, a rectory was always somewhere a little bit grand and serious, where you went to sip sherry or catch up on catechisms. It was not a place to jump into a canoe, paddle and swim, come back for a massage, laze in a sauna and then run out screaming half-naked to a bubbling hot-tub. But maybe I was visiting the wrong ones. This is, however, more my style of spiritual home. Most importantly, it is home to Julie and Patrick, and their three children, four horses and herd of cattle and, needless to say, it is no longer a rectory.

They offer bed and breakfast accommodation, all ingredients locally-sourced. The six bedrooms are furnished with an understated elegant style, boasting good old practical, rectory-esque mahogany, with no aspirations to grandeur. You might trip over one of their young son's toy helicopters in the grand sitting room overlooking the lake, much to the delight of my children, of course. If, however, you just want to fish and forget about people altogether, they also have a small one bedroom self-catering cottage, in one of the old stables.

But I love the main house, because it is a home. It is owned by people who love it so much, they came home from working in San Francisco to run it. Patrick and Julie explained that their years in San Francisco gave them a good grounding in eco-awareness, and so it was a natural progression for them to 'go green' when they started their business fourteen years ago. It was not easy to find low-energy light bulbs in Ireland at that time, but they persevered. Now with strict recycling and composting, use of only environmentally-friendly products, all electricity supplied by Airtricity, and almost half of their acreage

t: +353 (0) 71 964 4089
w: www.theoldrectoryireland.com

recently replanted with deciduous and spruce trees, they have deservedly been awarded the EU Flower accreditation certificate.

Patrick is currently building three self-catering apartments in the remaining disused stables, and is carefully considering renewable energy sources, so that he can take these buildings closer to carbon neutral status. Now all of that, plus maintaining a working farm, is worth raising a glass of sherry to.

Contact details
Address: The Old Rectory, Fenagh Glebe, Ballinamore, County Leitrim
Telephone: +353 (0) 71 964 4089
Website: www.theoldrectoryireland.com
Price: Single rooms €50-55 per person per night, double rooms €40-45 per person per night. Prices include breakfast and there is 25% reduction for children
Opening times: Bed and breakfast accommodation open from Easter to November. Self-catering open all year round
Disabled access: No wheelchair facilities

Getting there slowly
Take the train to Carrick-on-Shannon, and then it's a 23km cycle along the Kingfisher Cycle Trail to Fenagh (see pages 63-64). The nearest bus stop is in Ballinamore.

Drink at Quinn's
In Fenagh, Quinn's is a quick walk from the house – a favourite with the locals. The Abbey Bar in Fenagh is also great for music at weekends. If you are self-catering you can pick up organic vegetables at Willie's Vegetable shop in nearby Ballinamore, 5km away, as well as plenty of healthy supplies at the Nature Trail Health Store on the same street. It is also worth visiting the Farmers' Market at Carrick-on-Shannon, every Thursday 10am-2pm in the Market Yard.

Northern Ireland

Northern Ireland

Northern Ireland's leading environmental visitor attraction brings sustainability to life and gets to grips with the future of renewable energy and climate change. The Centre is built on formerly derelict farmland prone to flooding and now covers an expanse of transformed wetlands, woodland, grassland, ponds and lakes. The building houses Northern Ireland's largest selection of solar panels, with heating provided by a wood-burning boiler, using wood pellets.

This is a great day out for families. Entrance is free of charge and visitors can explore a multitude of interactive zones and nature-inspired activities. The first one that greeted us at the entrance involved mirrors and lights, which we had to adjust so that we could create enough energy to power some mini fans above our heads. It took a bit of time to get going, naturally, but we were all jumping up and down when they did actually start to move.

Outside, gluttonous litter bugs fed on visitors' recycled trash, but be careful, as certain bugs only take certain materials. There is a compost bin for the remains of your picnic lunch, and there are plenty of lovely places to sit by the water, letting the children delight in the many ducks and swans. Ecos Island has

t: +44 (0) 28 2566 4400
w: www.ballymena.gov.uk

been specifically set aside for feeding ducks, although my boys were slightly more into the miniature tractors than the Mallards. This is an ideal place for not only conserving energy but, in the case of my children, running some of it off, with walks over bridges, through the willow fairy ring, around the Ecos lake and alongside the Braid River.

If you really want to get into the Ecos ethos, you can cycle there on the National Cycle Network's Ecos Trail. This is a 27-km route between Ballymena and Glenarm, one of the nine Glens of Antrim, finally reaching the Antrim coast at Ballycastle.

Ecos Trail leaflets available from www.sustrans.org.uk

Contact details
Address: Ecos Millennium Environmental Centre, Kernohan's Lane, Broughshane Road, Ballymena, County Antrim BT43 7QA
Telephone: +44 (0) 28 2566 4400
Website: www.ballymena.gov.uk
Price: Entrance is free
Opening times: Monday-Friday 9am-5pm (last admissions 4pm), Saturday and Sunday 12pm-4pm during July and August only
Disabled access: Good facilities

Getting there slowly
Ride along the Ecos trail cycle route, National Cycle Network 97 (see www.sustrans.org), or take a bus or train to Ballymena, half an hour's walk from the Centre.

Rather like ships passing in the night, I was leaving the mainland at Ballycastle as Damien arrived off the ferry. "No bother," the host of the Manor House told me, "just let yourself in and make yourself at home. I'm just fetching some supplies".

The crossing to Rathlin was surprisingly choppy, and I later found out that the tides of Rathlin Sound play havoc with the waves as this is where the Atlantic and Irish Sea meet. The rugged little island gradually grows in size on a rising and falling horizon as the ferry makes its way to this remote and exposed place. I was glad to hop off the ferry, with lunch held down, where practically the first building I came across was the Manor House. Finding my key on the counter and settling into my room, I watched the ferry withdraw from the harbour with more passengers. Before the ferry was subsidised, the service linking Rathlin to the mainland was sporadic and unreliable. Now it's a crucial lifeline to the 70 or so permanent residents on the island. I realised that when an islander says that they're 'fetching supplies', what they come back with generally is what they can't rear, grow or catch themselves. This in itself means that little is wasted as it's an effort to get it there. Besides the islanders have gone to lengths to ensure the Council collect and recycle any rubbish after it was found that waste was going into the sea.

t: +44 (0) 28 2076 3964
w: www.rathlinmanorhouse.co.uk

When I caught up with Damien that

evening his next priority was dinner. In true island style, we went off to catch our meal. Jumping off the jetty and into Damien's speed boat, we dashed through the early evening currents in search of some sea bass or similar. The view of the cliff-faces was unparalleled as Damien advised me to look out for a family of inquisitive wild goats that greet passing sailors. Sadly the fish didn't bite that evening but we returned to the Manor House knowing that there was a piece of Rathlin Beef as back-up in the fridge.

It's easy to see why the Manor House is the first building you come across when you reach the island. It has played a huge role in the history of the island and, in more recent times, fell into the hands of the National Trust. Damien and his wife manage the building as a guesthouse. All the rooms are decorated tastefully and minimally to allow the seaviews through the windows to dominate. Damien has installed a recycling station, low-energy bulbs and solar panels to heat the water. Outside in the garden the couple grow their own produce which supplies their restaurant.

Damien's family, the McFauls, is one of the three main families to have lined the pages of the Rathlin history book over the years. The population of the island is so small that the chances of meeting one of the family during a trip are pretty high. After a conversation in the local pub with Damien's brother in the evening, I was shown around the RSPB site by his aunt the next day. Walking the long road to the South Lighthouse, it's no surprise that they are all fiercely proud of their island and visitors come, if not for the seabirds, then for the peace and quiet.

Contact details

Address: The Manor House, Rathlin Island, County Antrim BT54 6RT
Telephone: +44 (0) 28 2076 3964
Website:
www.rathlinmanorhouse.co.uk
Price: Single rooms from £30, doubles from £60
Opening times: Year round (group bookings only during the winter)
Disabled access: No access

Getting there slowly

From Belfast take the bus to Bally-mena, and then hop on a connecting service to Ballycastle. Get off at Marine Corner where you can catch the ferry to Rathlin Island (up to four sailings daily depending on the season). See www.calmac.co.uk/Rathlin for times and prices.

Visit the RSPB Centre

You should have your first encounter with Rathlin wildlife during the ferry cross-ing to the harbour. At certain times of the year the seabirds will circle above and in the water you may spot the odd seal or porpoise swimming the Causeway. The ferry doesn't take vehicles to the island without a permit, which means that all the tourists arrive by foot keeping traffic to an absolute minimum. Conse-quently, wildlife positively flourishes on Rathlin. Many visitors head to the RSPB Centre at the south of the island. Here you can find out more about the seabirds and watch them from a viewing platform next to the South Lighthouse. The Centre is open daily from 11am-3pm April to mid-September.
Website: www.rspb.org.uk

Portaferry is a small town on the Ards peninsula in County Down. It is one of those towns which you discover and wonder how it has remained hidden from the world for so long. With fishing boats, a car ferry which crosses the Lough to Strangford in minutes, views over the islands and coves, this truly merits its protected status as an Area of Outstanding Natural Beauty.

Equally hidden away behind Portaferry's tiny seafront is Exploris, Northern Ireland's aquarium. This does not aim to compete with international aquariums boasting shark-feeding sessions and whales dancing to music. It presents the underwater life of the Irish coastline and, in particular, the wide and varied marine ecosystem to be found only metres from its doors. These include mussels, crabs, juvenile Cod, Coley and Pollock. One of the most treasured species of Strangford Lough is the seal, many of which become orphaned or injured. The Aquarium started coming to the rescue of seal pups in 1989, feeding and nurturing them in a shed at the back of the aquarium. Ten years later, the Aquarium managed to get funding to build a sanctuary, with six quarantine pens, a food preparation room, a nursery pond and a large pond with underwater viewing area.

As this is a hospital, not a zoo, there are times of the year when you might not find any seals in care. If you want to be sure of seeing some of these adorable and, often still vulnerable, creatures, the hospital is at its busiest during the two pupping seasons. Common seals are born during June and July and grey seals between September and December. I was lucky to see three young ones, which were still being fed blended fish via a tube, as well as two which were almost ready to be released into the wild.

t: +44 (0) 28 4272 8062
w: www.exploris.org.uk

Luckily this small sanctuary was not hidden enough to escape the attention of the BBC, which supports a SealWatch programme on its website, where you can watch video footage of all the seals in their care. However, nothing beats a stroll or cycle out along the Ards Peninsula to see the real thing. You can also help fund Exploris' work through their Adopt-a-Seal programme.

See www.bbc.co.uk/northernireland/livingworld/sealwatch for SealWatch.

Contact details
Address: Exploris Aquarium, The Rope Walk, Castle Street, Portaferry, County Down BT22 1NZ
Telephone: +44 (0) 28 4272 8062
Website: www.exploris.org.uk
Price: Adult £7, Junior £4, Family £22, Seniors £4, Under fours free
Opening times: Open daily April to August, 10am-6pm Monday to Friday, 11am-6pm Saturday and 12pm-6pm Sunday. From September to March, open 10am-5pm Monday to Friday, 11am-5pm Saturday and 1pm-5pm Sunday
Disabled access: Good access

Getting there slowly
Take the bus from Belfast to Portaferry, or the bus to Strangford, and cross by ferry, which takes fifteen minutes. During operating hours the ferry leaves Portaferry at quarter to and quarter past the hour; and Strangford on the hour and half past the hour. For ferry information, telephone +44 (0) 28 4488 1637.

Eat at the Portaferry Hotel
If the evening meals are as good as the huge heap of smoked salmon I had in the bar at lunchtime, then I might have to check in next time. I loved the intimate atmosphere in this hotel, obviously favoured by many of the locals. You can down your lunchtime tipple as you watch the ferry leave the shores of Strangford, ready to catch it on the way back over.
Address: The Portaferry Hotel, The Strand, Portaferry, County Down BT22 1PE
Telephone: +44 (0) 28 427 28231
Website: www.portaferryhotel.com

Cycle to Castleward
Take your bike on the ferry and cycle to Castleward, one of the National Trust's most impressive estates in Northern Ireland. A 1.5km section of path has recently been upgraded by Sustrans to allow walkers and cyclists to access the estate. This links with the internal estate roads, which bring walkers and cyclists along the loughshore, as well as feeding into the Strangford Lough Cycle Trail, a 150km signed circular cycle route on quiet country roads. For details and a map, see www.sustrans.org.uk.

The name given to the mountain range, the Mournes, suggests a sad desolate place. Nothing could be further from the truth. My heart literally skipped a beat as I opened the curtains of my eco-loft apartment at Tory Bush Cottages. It was worth arriving in darkness, just to be able to watch the sun rise over the heather, moss and bog-covered valleys as well as the piney peaks of nearby Tollymore Forest Park. They looked like school text book images of glacial formations, with the crags and crevices slowly revealing themselves as shafts of light pushed through the morning mist. No wonder this area is being muted for National Park status.

Having all this as its 'back garden' is top of the list of Tory Bush's green credentials. It's a pretty good start, although David Maginn, the owner, is a firm devotee to the sustainable tourism movement and has made huge efforts towards keeping his little piece of the Mournes as green as possible. The cottages are all built in the local 'clachan' style, with whitewashed walls and slate roofs. In the main reception and adjoining 'eco-loft', he has used sustainable building techniques. "Insulating with sheep's wool brings money to other farmers like me. It makes sense", said David.

This enterprising farmer also boasts a solar panel to heat the water and a rain recovery system to do the laundry for the entire complex. He also uses recycled cardboard plasterboard, and a wood pellet boiler. Only the eco-loft runs on renewable energy at the moment, but David is constantly looking at ways of developing this, to make all the cottages as sustainable as possible. However, just being able to walk out the door, and access the mountain

t: +44 (0) 28 4372 4348
w: www.torybush.com

trails almost immediately makes this hideout in the hills the perfect green place to start as you mean to go on. If the National Park status goes ahead, let's hope other landowners in the area can be inspired by David Maginn's continuing efforts to protect the treasure on his doorstep.

Contact details
Address: Tory Bush Cottages, 79 Tullyree Road, Bryansford, Newcastle, County Down BT34 5LD
Telephone: +44 (0) 28 4372 4348
Website: www.torybush.com
Price: Eco-loft (with one double room) from £130 for two-night stay
Opening times: All year round
Disabled access: The Eco-loft is not suitable for wheelchair users as access is via steep stairs. Some of the other cottages have wheelchair access and most have downstairs bedrooms and bathrooms

Getting there slowly
There are regular buses from Belfast to Newcastle, and it's an eight kilometre taxi journey to Tory Bush Cottages. There are less regular services from Belfast and Newcastle to Bryansford Village, just under three kilometres from the cottages. Tory Bush's sister company, Mourne Cycle Tours will deliver bikes to the cottages. See www.mournecycletours.com or phone +44 (0) 28 4372 4348.

Eat and drink at the Maghera Inn
Maghera Inn is six kilometres from the cottages and winner of Northern Ireland's Pub of the Year award in 2007. The beef and Guinness pie will revive you after a day's walking and, if you go on the first Friday of the month, you'll catch local traditional musicians in session.
Address: The Maghera Inn, 86 Ballyloughlin Rd, Castlewellan, County Down BT31 9HE
Telephone: +44 (0) 28 437 22236
Website: www.themagherainn.com

This one-woman company is Loretto Coyle, one of those invaluable, and under-publicised people working in tourism. The local guide. I have always considered myself far too independent a traveller to need the services of a local guide, until I met Loretto. And now, I seek them out whenever I travel. I met her on a trip to the Mourne Mountains in County Down where, travelling alone, and with a limited amount of time to brush up my ordnance survey skills, I went in search of necessary guidance. So, one early morning (I would still have been in bed were it not for an early appointment with Loretto), the mist hovering over the mountains, and my eyelids still a little heavy, I donned my boots and awaited her arrival at my accommodation.

Loretto, a Blue Badge guide, arrived bang on time, with a smile as big as her enthusiasm for sharing her vast local knowledge. She handed me a much better daypack than the one I had with me, some snacks, walking poles, and took out her laminated map. When she asked, "Do you want to follow The Ulster Way?" I had a slight panic that politics were already on the agenda. But then I remembered that it is in fact a designated walking route around Northern Ireland. "Are we allowed to deviate from the Ulster Way?" I asked, and Loretto smiled knowingly. "We can go anywhere we want; this ground is open to everyone." Somehow, it always feels easier to deviate when you know you have a local to reassure you of the boundaries.

We took on a half-day walk, although Loretto does full-day guiding, on foot or bike. She doesn't limit herself to the Mournes either, leading cycling tours

t: +44 (0) 28 4372 5191
w: www.outdoorirelandnorth.co.uk

around Strangford Lough or Downpatrick, to name a few. Today we were taking on the slopes of Slieve Loughshannagh. Loretto pointed out swathes of peat bog, its white bog cotton flowers, several varieties of moss (some as smooth velvet black as Guinness itself) and identified the various peaks. We stopped to traverse the Mourne Wall. Twenty-two miles long, this is a dry-stone wall which connects 15 summits including Donard, and Commedagh. The local water

authority commissioned it in 1904 to enclose 9,000 acres draining down to two reservoirs, the Silent Valley and Ben Crom and it must be one of Ireland's greatest building feats. Loretto answered all my questions, geographical, geological, historical and political. Nothing fazed her. She seemed happy to walk at my pace, despite being capable of taking on two peaks in the time it took me to get halfway up one, stopping to chat whenever it suited. Without her, I would not only have got lost, but I would have resisted the challenge of some of the hills she knew so well. I would also not have learnt so much, nor laughed so much. If this is the Ulster Way, way to go, I say.

For information on other guides in Ireland, see www.bluebadgeireland.org and the Federation of Irish Guiding Interests, telephone +353 (0) 1 278 1626, www.tourguides.ie.

Contact details
Address: Outdoor Ireland North, 14 Shimnavale, Newcastle, County Down BT33 0EF
Telephone: +44 (0) 28 4372 5191
Website: www.outdoorirelandnorth.co.uk
Price: Half-day guided walks from £15 per person (minimum group 4 persons). Price negotiable for individuals

A bed and breakfast is a simple notion. But there is nothing simple about this one, with its fine linen sheets and five star organic breakfasts. So far, it wins the top prize for eco-breakfast. It was the apple and blackcurrants soaked in elderberry juice, served with Anna's home-made yoghurt that did it. Or maybe the organic apricots marinated in ginger syrup. Or the freshly-made warm scones. They all merge into one memory of gastronomic gorgeousness.

If you can tear yourself away from the long breakfast table, where all guests gather as a family to share the many stories of our hosts, Anna and Ken, you can also feast your eyes on some architectural feats in their recent extension. Like I said, nothing is simple here. A vast construction of steel and glass, which pays tribute to the lake at the bottom of the garden, houses not only the most spectacular living space I have seen in a B&B, but also the most eclectic interior design. Italian candelabras, a grand piano, a tapered steel staircase, local artwork, and minstrels' galleries leading up to more beautifully furnished guest bedrooms. From there, you can wander through their two acres of flower gardens, shrubberies and copses, obviously landscaped and maintained with devotion, as there is a sculpted bust of the gardener in one of the many hidden corners.

t: +44 (0) 28 975 41566
w: www.annashouse.com

All of this created by Anna and Ken, whose commitment to the environment (there are solar panels, geothermal heating, low-energy light-bulbs and an organic kitchen garden) is from the heart. And Ken likes to discuss energy saving to the very last nanowatt, with Anna stepping in at regular intervals with offerings of more delicious food. She confessed to not being as 'green' as she would like. "I need my linen to be clean, you see, and I am not sure about the eco-friendly washing powders getting the best results." In lots of ways, this is Anna to a tee. Everything is done to perfection. I think that will always be a feature of Anna's House, no matter what washing powder she chooses. So hopefully, she will take the risk.

Contact details
Address: Anna's House, Tullynagee, 35 Lisbarnett Road, Comber, Newtownards, County Down BT23 6AW
Telephone: +44 (0) 28 975 41566
Website: www.annashouse.com
Price: Single rooms from £50 and doubles from £80
Opening times: Open all year except Christmas and New Year
Disabled access: One ground floor guest room is fully equipped for wheelchair access

Getting there slowly
Take a bus from Belfast to Killinchy and get off at Lisbane. The house is about a kilometre walk from the bus stop. Or you can cycle from Belfast taking the traffic-free Comber Greenway from the Belfast suburbs (about 15km).

Cycle the Comber Greenway
The Comber Greenway is a new 12 km traffic-free section of the National Cycle Network being developed by Sustrans along the old Belfast to Comber railway line. Although many sections are already open to walkers and cyclists, it is due for completion in September 2008. It provides a tranquil green corridor all the way from Comber (five kilometres from Anna's house) to East Belfast.
Website: www.combergreenway.org.uk

"Leave no trace" is Jerome O'Loughlin's motto. He works by it, lives by it, drives by it and teaches it. That doesn't mean he doesn't like to be noticed. Our kids had spent an hour wailing "I don't want to go on a bus tour", until Jerome turned up at our door. The sight of his bright-green minibus, with pictures of hikers and bikers emblazoned on the side, stopped us, and everyone who was passing by, in our tracks. Especially when they noticed the sign: "Powered by vegetable oil".

This biofuel bus is run on pure plant oil extracted from Irish-grown and processed rapeseed. Jerome, the owner of Ireland Eco Tours, trained guide, and expert in ecotourism, mountain biking, surfing, hiking, local history, geography and geology, wins my vote for most innovative 'ecoescap-er'. In his mean green machine, he offers guided tours to places of eco-interest in Leitrim, Fermanagh, Sligo, Cavan and Donegal. He has run, cycled and hiked just about all of these backroads, it would seem, so no better man for showing you the real Ireland, steering well away from the ever-expanding national road networks.

Jerome offers longer Multi-Sport seven day packages, but we opted for a one-day eco-tour, perfect for families. Jerome needs to fill the bus to make these trips viable, but with two families staying together in The Old Schoolhouse in Cavan (see pages 46-48), there were plenty of us. First stop was Castle Archdale Country Park in Fermanagh. In between nature lessons in this stunning reserve, Jerome had us all enthralled with stories of WW2 flying boats. The RAF

t: +44 (o) 28 686 59171
w: www.irelandecotours.com

used this as a training base, enabling pilots to sweep down the Lough Erne corridors in preparation for the real thing. He pointed across the Lough to the heights of Lough Navar, where two airmen perished, when their plane crashed into the cliffs.

The children were eating every word out of Jerome's hands at this point, and there were no complaints as we hopped back on board for another nature reserve. We stopped in Belcoo for lunch, with the indefatigable Jerome being questioned non-stop at this stage by children and adults alike. We walked off the Customs House restaurant's exceptional desserts in Correl Glen Nature Reserve. This, like all the others en route, was unknown to me before meeting Jerome. He skilfully guided us up twisting paths lined with indigenous Oaks, Ashes and Elms, along grassy banks full of wild garlic, past gushing waterfalls and more playful streams, stopping to point out interesting sites en route.

Jerome may have won my children's award for eco-cool, but anyone who can keep my children (and adults) entertained, educated and enjoying three different nature reserves, deserves a fleet of eco-buses to his name. Our most unexpectedly uplifting day ended, appropriately, back across the lake from where we started – approximately 1,000 feet up at the Lough Navar viewpoint, from the top of the Cliffs of Magho. We took in the view down the corridor which had been taken by those wartime airline pilots, along the River Erne all the way out to Donegal Bay in the distance. The children had gone off quietly in search of the memorials to the two airmen who had died, and we all ended the day in a quiet meditative silence, looking across invisible borders into counties Fermanagh, Tyrone and Donegal. This is the home Jerome wants to share with visitors. He succeeded in the greenest and most generous way possible.

Contact details

Address: Ireland Eco Tours, Corry, Belleek, County Fermanagh BT93 3FU
Telephone: +44 (0) 28 686 59171
Website: www.irelandecotours.com
Price: £25 per person for a day tour. For packages, see website for details
Disabled access: No wheelchair facilities

This state-of-the-art yoga retreat, with airy studio, underheated wooden floors, treatment rooms, sauna and hot tub is the work of a farmer, single mother and the best masseur I have come across in years. Gabriele, owner of Blaney Spa and adjoining Innish Beg cottages, gave up farming some time ago, but did not want to lose contact with the Fermanagh landscape she loves so dearly. That is why everything here looks out on Fermanagh's lakelands. Stretch out for a massage and look out over the lake. Have an early morning yoga session, on the decked veranda, also overlooking the lake. I took a two-minute walk from the front door of my traditional whitewashed cottage, cup of coffee in hand, to watch the sun come up over the lake. You can have all the hot tubs and saunas in the world, but nothing beats diving in off the jetty. That heals just about everything.

Gabriele was quick to explain my cottage's one-star Tourist Board accreditation, (although the other two cottages have three stars). These are the original stone farm cottages, refurbished by Gabriele fifteen years ago, and the one-bedroom loft cottage I was staying in has had little done to it since then. That may worry the tourist boards, but it didn't worry me. Personally, I found the coin-operated electricity metre rather quaint, and a brilliant 70s solution to saving energy. They are reasonably priced and accreditation isn't everything. The 'fairy wood-land walk' from the cottage to the jetty on the lake's shore, the rowing boat with oars poised for use and the wild orchids and strawberries scenting the misty air upgraded it to five star for me anyway.

If you want modern, you only have to walk up the hill to the spa. Gabriele offers many residential weekend work-shops, from mid-week holistic breaks

t: +44 (0) 28 6864 1525
w: www.blaneyspaandyogacentre.com

to yoga and art weekends. Painting in the hot tub, now there's a thought. This is not a place to worry about one, two, or three-star accommodation. This is a place to enjoy the peace of Lough Erne, some healing treatments, and the company of a woman who has achieved the creation of one of the most simple and comfy retreats in Fermanagh.

Contact details
Address: Blaney Spa and Yoga Centre, Innishbeg, Blaney, Enniskillen, County Fermanagh BT93 7EP
Telephone: +44 (0) 28 6864 1525
Website: www.blaneyspaandyogacentre.com and www.innishbegcottages.com
Price: Small Cottage £180-300 per week, £120 weekends. Large Cottage £420-630 per week, £240 weekends. Art and yoga weekends from £295
Opening times: Cottages available all year round
Disabled access: The large cottage and spa both have wheelchair access

Getting there slowly
Take the bus to Enniskillen, and from there Blaney is an 11km taxi ride.

Go cheese-making
Take a Sunday course in cheese-making at nearby Corleggy Farm. Instead of bringing your own bottle, you bring your own bucket. A bucket, a ladel and an apron are all you need to partake in a day of cheese-making at Corleggy Summer Cheese School, about 35km from Blaney. It's a day-long course which sends you back home (with your bucket) and your own one kilo of cows' milk cheese. Course costs €150, including organic lunch, and wine.
Address: Corleggy Farm, Corleggy, Belturbet, County Cavan
Telephone: +353 (0) 49 952 2930
Website: www.corleggy.com

I grew up in 70's and 80's Belfast at a time when there wasn't a lot of sharing going on. I remember 'Share' when it was established in 1981, as a haven of goodness in a world of strife, where disadvantaged children, catholic and protestant, disabled and able-bodied went on holiday together. I didn't get the chance to go then, so was relieved to see that it is still there all these years later. I was even more relieved to see that its flag of democracy and accessibility is still flying high.

I didn't need a map for this one, as I was guided by the three windmills towering over Upper Lough Erne, where Share nestles into the shoreline. The wind turbines supply electricity to the holiday village, but even more impressive, are the three wood pellet boilers which heat the chalets, swimming pool and arts arena. Pellets are from a local producer, and all guaranteed to be from renewable forests. Combined with the reed bed system and four solar water heating systems, it is not surprising that the Village is often the focus of educational visits. It can, and does, willingly, share its experience of running such a large visitor centre on renewables. It now boasts the use of 99 per cent renewable electricity and heat.

Despite all this work and commitment to caring for the environment, (it also has EU Flower accreditation, so recycling, composting, and eco-friendly cleaning products are par for the course at this stage), its primary focus is people. It caters for groups of young and old in fully residential activity weeks, at very accessible prices. Self-catering chalets are fairly basic, but Share is not striving towards a five-star eco-break, and the feel is more bunkhouse than boutique hotel. But they are ideal for families, with copious amounts of activities, arts and sports, available to self-catering guests as well as groups. From kayaking to pottery, sail-

t: +44 (0) 28 6772 2122
w: www.sharevillage.org

ing to singing, they cater for everyone here. Take a trip on the Inishcruiser, which is moored at Share's marina. This two-hour cruise takes in many of the hidden spots on Lough Erne's intricate web of islands, including Crom Castle Estate, home to Lord Erne. Everyone is part of the community here and, somehow, they show that this sharing business really does work.

Contact details
Address: Share Holiday Village, Smith's Strand, Lisnaskea, County Fermanagh BT92 0EQ
Telephone: +44 (0) 28 6772 2122
Website: www.sharevillage.org
Price: £180 for a winter weekend break to £590 for a peak season week-long break. Activities cost extra
Opening times: Closed for two weeks over Christmas and New Year
Disabled access: All of Share's facilities have been purpose-built for guests with disabilities

Getting there slowly
Take a bus from Dublin or Belfast to Enniskillen. From here there is a bus connection to Lisnaskea. Share Village is four miles from Lisnaskea, and you can call a taxi here (telephone +44 (0) 28 6772 2360 for CDM Cabs). Other taxis are available from Enniskillen bus station, a 19km journey.

Eat at the Cherry Tree
Lisnaskea is not really the epicurean centre of Ireland, but Northern Ireland is famous for its selection of breads, and the Cherry Tree is a fantastic home bakery to stock up on soda farls, potato bread, wheaten bread, scones, pancakes and fruit sodas. This is a family-run business, which prides itself on sourcing as many of its ingredients, including sandwich fillings from its deli counter, in the Fermanagh region. If you're on the road and fancy a break, it is also worth stopping at the Coach Inn in Maguiresbridge, with an open fire and a very friendly welcome.
Address: The Cherry Tree, 107-109 Main Street, Lisnaskea, County Fermanagh
Telephone: +44 (0) 28 6772 1571
Website: www.wheresmywheaten.com

Charles Plunkett who manages this estate on behalf of The Duke of Abercorn, has done a green and good thing. He replaced an oil burning boiler, with running costs of £22,000 a year for the castle alone, with a state-of-the-art wood pellet burner, which uses locally sourced fuel. As it sleeps fourteen, you can split the bill but you do need a big 'cast' for what feels like the set of a period drama, although more authentic in its aristocratic eccentricities. "We have 950 paintings around the estate," Charles said, able to identify each and every one.

But however green his heart is, Charles does not have access to the purse strings. Not only are the courtyard apartments, cottages and lodges still on oil, but there are few other signs of environmentally sensitive practices, although they do have wood-burning stoves, with an option to turn off the oil. What Charles does do, however, is contribute hugely to the preservation of some of Fermanagh's most undeniably precious natural heritage. Belle Isle is indeed a 'beautiful island', on the northern tip of Upper Lough Erne. The estate, and working farm, is a designated Area of Special Scientific Interest. Walking the hills and shores was like one big nature lesson, as I tried to identify the wide variety of old Irish trees, including huge Horse Chestnuts, Beech, Ash and Yew. The birdlife was so abundant that on my early morning walk, the dawn chorus didn't ever seem to stop.

But they have got the green ball rolling, especially in the kitchen. Chef Liz Moore runs a cookery school on the grounds, teaching with a slow food ethos, and sourcing produce locally. Within four years, she will be able to source her fruit in the walled garden, where Charles has planted a vast orchard. Now all the Duke has to do is sell a few paintings and he could convert the rest of the place to a truly green and beautiful Island.

t: +44 (0) 28 6638 7231
w: www.belleisle-estate.com

Contact details

Address: Belle Isle Estate, Lisbellaw, Enniskillen, County Fermanagh BT94 5HG
Telephone: +44 (0) 28 6638 7231
Website: www.belleisle-estate.com
Price: Apartments from £370 per week, coach house from £383 per week, and castle from £2,310 per week
Opening times: All year round
Disabled access: One of the courtyard apartments is designed to be totally wheelchair-friendly, and one of the boats available to hire is designed for easy access by wheelchair users. The kitchen in the cookery school is also suitable for wheelchair users

Getting there slowly

Take the bus to Enniskillen and taxi to Belle Isle (about £12). It is a hilly 15km cycle from Belle Isle into Enniskillen. You can rent bikes from Wild Flower Cycling Holidays (in Cavan) who will also deliver them to the estate (see www.wildflowercyclingholidays.com for details).

Shop at O'Doherty's Black Bacon

I went in search of a restaurant and met Pat O'Doherty, the butcher along the way. He owns O'Doherty's Black Bacon, and recently bought an island in Lough Erne to rear his pigs in the open. Specially cured with no added water or phosphates, this is the real thing. If you are staying in Fermanagh, and are a meat-eater, it's the place to stock up for the week. If you time it well, you can pick up some of his freshly picked wild mushrooms to go with your award-winning burgers. I loved his shop so much that I skipped the restaurant and left with dinner from his place instead. Ingredients: one locally-sourced wild venison steak, bag of organic pasta, organic garlic and tomatoes.
Address: O'Doherty's Black Bacon, Belmore Street, Enniskillen, County Fermanagh
Telephone: +44 (0) 28 6632 2152
Website: www.blackbacon.com

Unlike many activity centres, Corralea is delightfully intimate. It feels more like the home of some very cool friend – the one with all the best toys in town. Water trampolines and slides, canoes, a climbing wall, windsurfing boards and a load of bikes. I even tried my hand at archery, under the careful guidance of Marius who, with his wife, Isabelle, entertains and teaches families, youth groups and anyone in search of some outdoor fun on Lough Macnean in Fermanagh.

There are six cottages overlooking the Lough, four of which have solar panels, and all have wood-burning stoves, with endless supplies of wood sourced from Corralea's predominantly Birch woodland. All cottages have been accredited by the EU Flower eco-label for their minimal impact on the environment. I found the cottages a little stark and functional, but this does not matter, because Corralea is about the outdoors. All the activities here are non-motor based, and while the children were jumping into the Lough at the bottom of the garden, I could take off to a quieter spot with my canoe. But as Marius is a family man, he understands that sometimes you want to do things 'en famille', so he will plan activities to suit your family's interests too. Or you can leave the kids to it, as long as they are over nine years old. I recommend the all-day cycle around the Lough, hopping over the border to the Cavan Burren, and head into the Ballintempo Forest, along the Ulster Way walking trail. Order an excellent map of the Lough area from www.visitmacnean.com in advance or Marius will give you a copy on arrival.

Corralea offers two innovative weekend packages, and has recently been awarded Greenbox accreditation (see pages 61-62). One of these packages is "Mountain bike away, and canoe home", which involves cycling with a guide through

t: +44 (0) 28 6638 6123
w: www.activityireland.com

extensive forest trails and along the Lough shore, stopping for lunch and then paddling back to base. These are not aimed at lycra-clad loonies, just a day outdoors, taking things at a pace to suit all levels of fitness. The other package is underground, exploring the area's caves, rock formations and hydrology, with a qualified cave leader. So, if you are donning a cycling or a caving helmet, or just want to sit by the Lough and watch the young ones get on with it, Corralea accommodates and welcomes one and all.

Contact details
Address: Corralea Activity Centre, Belcoo, County Fermanagh BT93 5DZ
Telephone: +44 (0) 28 6638 6123
Website: www.activityireland.com
Price: 4-5 person cottage between £210 and £340 per week, depending on the season. 6 person cottage, £320-550 per week. Activities range between £9-18 for half a day for residents. Canoe and bike hire is from £10
Opening times: All year round, but activities are limited in winter months
Disabled access: One cottage is fully equipped for wheelchair users

Getting there slowly
Take the bus from Belfast or Enniskillen to Belcoo. Taxi or walk 5km to Corralea. There is also a rural bus service serving the West of Fermanagh called the Rural Rover. This is a very cheap door-to-door service but must be booked 24 hours in advance (telephone +44 (0) 28 6632 0599).

Visit the Marble Arch Caves
The most spectacular caves in the area can be found at the Marble Arch Caves European Geopark. The guides have a wonderful sense of pride in this, one of Europe's finest show caves, leading you along underground rivers in an electrically-powered boat, or along the complex structure of walkways, to see the glistening stalactites and enormous caverns of this superb subterranean world. The caves may close in severe weather, so always call in advance before visiting. Open from mid-March to September, seven days a week.
Address: Marble Arch Caves European Geopark, Marlbank, Florencecourt, County Fermanagh BT92 1EW
Telephone: +44 (0) 28 663 48855
Website: www.marblearchcaves.net

Just follow the smoke signals over County Fermanagh to the best eco-camping in Ireland. They will lead you to a tipi on Orchard Acre Farm, where we all tucked up under a traditional North American Indian canvas, with wood-burning brazier as its centre piece. Here, Teresa O'Hare, who runs this exquisite ecoescape, has carefully crafted the perfect recipe for incorporating her passions in life: cooking, hospitality and Fermanagh.

There is one tipi, ideal for a family of four or five. This is not tipi-chic, but good earthy camping, with gravel surface, gas-burning stove, but all done in a cute and thoughtful way. The fire (an inspired recycled washing machine drum), rapidly became the focal point, as we constantly adjusted the canvas flaps to ensure the smoke escaped. Hugh, Teresa's husband, explained how the "tell-tale" ribbons, hanging off the locally-harvested tipi poles, show the wind direction. He was an expert at showing which way to roll back the flaps, so that we weren't all choking inside our adorable abode. It really worked, and we woke up to glowing embers.

As if this wasn't enough excitement for our two young boys, they got to bottle feed the pet lamb, collect eggs, harvest rhubarb from the kitchen garden, and forage for wild garlic on the banks of the brook which does, indeed, babble through the farm. We left mucky, smoky and extremely happy. And with a home-made rhubarb tart, which the boys made in Teresa's cookery class. If you fancy it, and we did, she lays on all sorts of extra activities, from cooking and gardening, to basket weaving in the eco-barn.

You can book a basic package, which includes accommodation and an organic hamper of local bacon, farm eggs, Irish cheeses and breads and Teresa's home-made soup. The deluxe package has all food and activities of your choice included. The only thing left to do was discover Fermanagh. As this is the Lakeland of Ulster, and this is a tipi holiday, the best way to travel was by canoe. We cycled to nearby Castle Archdale Country Park, and there it

t: +44 (0) 28 6862 1066
w: www.orchardacrefarm.com

was, moored up and ready to go. The icing on the cake made from the best O'Hare ingredients for a perfect family holiday.

Contact details
Address: Orchard Acre Farm, Moynaghan North Road, Lisnarick, Irvinestown, County Fermanagh BT94 1LQ
Telephone: +44 (0) 28 6862 1066
Website: www.orchardacrefarm.com
Price: For four people a weekend basic package costs £240 (week £660). Deluxe weekend package £400 (week £950). Packed lunches £5.90 per person, and evening dinner £12.50 per person
Opening times: Weather-depending, the tipi is up from Easter to September but there are courses and workshops all year round at Orchard Acre Farm
Disabled access: Barn and workshops are designed for wheelchair access, but the tipi is not suitable for wheelchair users due to uneven surface and low beds

Getting there slowly
Take the bus from Enniskillen to Pettigo – there are three per day. They stop at the end of the road up to Orchard Acre Farm, which is only four minutes walk away. You can also take a bus from Enniskillen to Irvinestown, which is 3.5km from the farm.

Visit Oghill Farm
Oghill Farm is the HQ of Ireland's finest and creamiest ice cream, Tickety Moo. If you come at around 5pm, you can watch the impressive herd of Jersey cows being brought in to be milked. They have installed a viewing gallery to encourage consumers to gain a greater understanding of the source of their top-quality ingredients. This is a great family excursion, topped off with a purchase of the final product, which comes in eighteen different flavours. If you are there in summer, go for the Balmy Strawberry. They use Orchard Acre's strawbs and balsamic vinegar.
Website: www.tickety-moo.com

I got lost on my way to Little Crom, finding myself in the middle of 'Big Crom'. The latter is the home of Lord Erne and the vast National Trust Crom Estate. The former is the home of cattle and turkey farmer, Damien O'Keefe. He kindly came out to meet me, and the first thing he did was drive me around 'Big Crom', genuinely proud to have it as his neighbour. I think Lord Erne should be equally as proud to have Damien as his, because when he led me down to the water's edge at Little Crom I quickly saw that size doesn't matter. It's the Lough that matters, and you can't get much closer to it and all its natural finery, than at his cottages.

Nothing beat the early-morning spin on one of Damien's wooden Burke boats and Upper Lough Erne is virtually traffic-free. One good thing to come out of the years of conflict in Northern Ireland was that such areas were left untouched by tourism at a time when the industry was destroying other parts of the island. I took the boat out through the reeds, past Mute Swans, Moorhens and Coots. If you don't spot a Kingfisher, you can head off on the nearby Kingfisher Trail cycle route (see pages 63-64) and spend a day searching for one. You don't need to go far on the boat or bike to find a perfect picnic spot either, as Little Crom overlooks Galloon Island, where I found an ancient burial ground from an old monastery. You don't even need the outboard motor for this trip. It is so close even I could row it.

t: +44 (0) 28 6773 8074
w: www.littlecromcottages.com

The cottages are comfortable and spacious, with oak and slate flooring, wood-burning stoves, and hot water powered by solar panels to warm you up after some lake swimming. Damien has been awarded EU Flower status, and gives plenty of instructions on how to be environmentally–friendly. But as a farmer diversifying into tourism, who provides bikes and three boats, free of charge, on one of the most beautiful Special Protection Areas in Ireland, Damien needs neither title nor certificate to show off his green status.

Contact details

Address: Little Crom Cottages,
29 Clones Road, Newtownbutler,
County Fermanagh BT92 6SB
Telephone: +44 (0) 28 6773 8074
Website: www.littlecromcottages.com
Price: From £175 for a weekend in
low season to £525 for a week in
high season
Opening times: All year round
Disabled access: Excellent access, with ramps and wheelchair-friendly
bathroom facilities

Getting there slowly

Take a bus from Enniskillen to Clones, with connections from Belfast and get off at Newtownbutler. The cottages are 4km from the town, and the local taxi firm is VR Taxis, telephone +44 (0) 28 6773 8999.

Explore the Crom Estate

Cycle, walk or boat to the National Trust's Crom Estate, where you can also have snacks in the coffee shop. You pay £6 to moor at the Visitor Centre and have all day to stroll around the 2,000 acres. This is one of the National Trust's most magnificent nature reserves, boasting the largest surviving oak woodland in Northern Ireland, as well as its 800-year-old Yew trees. The Castle is closed to the public, but you are in the right area, as Fermanagh is also home to two of the National Trust's other fine mansions at Castle Coole and Florence Court, both of which are on the Kingfisher Cycle Trail.
Address: Crom, Upper Lough Erne, Newtownbutler, County Fermanagh BT92 8AP
Telephone: +44 (0) 28 6773 8118
Website: www.nationaltrust.org.uk

Paddy Jones is a farmer, canoeist, caver and green entrepreneur. It's all go for Paddy, and he doesn't let his clients sit still for a minute either. I took one of his canoes down the River Sillees in Fermanagh, where I didn't pass another human being for the three hours I was out on the water. Paddy had told me the local story about Saint Faber who cursed the River Sillees, making it flow up against the hill. That was a good enough excuse to go for a gentle three hour canoe down (or up) river, rather than taking on the fifteen kilometres from Boho to its source in Lough Erne. "I'll meet you at the third bridge after the island", he said, where I swapped canoe for bike, to cycle back to base. I thought he might make me jog home for my supper, but there is no triathalon training needed here. Just a willingness to discover the ins and outs, ups and downs of Ireland's famous lakelands. Best bit of the cycle was through the Belmore Forest, where I came across a waterfall which has gouged out a deep pothole in the limestone. This is known locally as "Pollnagollum". Irish for "Hole of the Doves". Beware of the slippery steps leading down to the foot of the waterfall, from where you can see inside a large cave, previously used in Victorian times as a show cave. Locals don't recommend exploring this one, unless with experienced cavers.

Paddy is an expert caver, and font of local knowledge. If he is not too busy, he is available as a local guide and, with the most natural storytelling skills, he shared his vast range of local myths, knowledge of the local natural heritage and impressive cultural insight. It's all done with great humour and a generosity of spirit.

t: +44 (0) 28 6772 2992
w: www.bohoecohire.com

Perhaps it is because this area was badly hit during the years of conflict in

Northern Ireland but these waterways, hills and forests of Fermanagh are still so unknown to visitors. I doubt if too many Northern Irish people have canoed the Sillees either. Farmers like Paddy, who are keen to diversify into tourism and who do it out of such a genuine love of their homeland, are still rare. Let's hope that the government does all it can to support green tourism initiatives like this. Paddy is also planning to build two ecohouses, so watch this space for developments.

Contact details
Address: Boho EcoHire, Corr Bridge, Boho, County Fermanagh
Telephone: +44 (0) 780 190 8076 or +44 (0) 28 6772 2992
Website: www.bohoecohire.com
Price: Canoe hire £30 per day, £20 half-day; Bicycle hire, £15 per day; Guiding services £20 per hour, £70 per day
Opening times: All year round
Disabled access: No wheelchair facilities

Getting there slowly
Boho is on The Kingfisher Cycle Trail (see pages 76-77). Take a bus from Enniskillen to Derrygonnelly (5km away) or Monea (3.5km away).

Drink at the Linnet Inn
Linnet Inn is a thatched pub, which sat waiting for me like a picture postcard at Tullyhommon, where I climbed up the river bank at the end of my canoe trip, to meet Paddy and his trailer. You can't indulge too much as you have to cycle back again, but you'll get a cup of tea and a warm fire before you hit the road.

The Sperrins region of Northern Ireland is a designated Area of Outstanding Natural Beauty, and one which should be shouted about more from the hilltops. It certainly has enough of them, as this is one of the largest upland areas in Ireland. Although I am not sure how many people will hear the shouts, as this unspoilt landscape of blanket bog and heatherclad slopes seems to go on, uninterrupted, for ever.

The Central Sperrins Way is a 40km circular walk around the interior of this spectacular landscape, and there is no better place to base yourself for exploring it than at the heart of the region in Omagh. One family who really knows how to live life to the full in Omagh is the Fyffes, who run this independent hostel on their small organic farm. They work the farm, have children, second jobs, run festivals, are active community group members, hike, bike, and were digging up a field to build a reed bed waste system when I was there. And yet they both managed to pick me up at Omagh bus station, with big smiley welcomes, whisking me into a frenzied excitement over all that their county had to offer.

The Fyffes know County Tyrone like the back of their hands. Marella is an orienteering expert and, if there is a big enough group staying, it won't be hard to persuade her to take you out for a run. She put me through my paces in the Gortin Glens, panting my way through some of the 4,000 acres of lush coniferous forest. Luckily, her expert guidance kept me from getting totally

t: +44 (0) 28 8224 1973
w: www.omaghhostel.co.uk

disorientated by the endless towers of Sitka and Norway Spruces.

The Omagh Hostel should be carbon neutral by 2009, boasting the use of a biomass boiler, planting over twenty trees a year to offset any surplus. This year they have replanted a completely new woodland of 900 indigenous trees. They recycle everything: "My pigs are the best recycling bin", said Marella, "there is a lot of waste food at the hostel, such as pasta and bread, which is hard to compost. But the pigs love it". They also love having their tummies tickled, apparently, and that's a trick you aren't taught in many hostels around the world. After a day I felt like one of the family. This is hostel life as it should be; plain and simple, with clean comfortable rooms, and great value. It is a warm and friendly place to crash, after a day's walking or cycling. For walking, they have an impressive list of local guides on their website and, for cycling, Omagh is one of the main links to the Sustrans Cycle Route 92.

© Lesley Bulman

The highlight of my trip was in the Gortin Glens. We climbed to the point where the Pollan Burn stream tumbles down the hillside in a magnificent water fall. Watching the dragon and damselflies flirt madly through the rainbows, I was able to breathe in the peace and calm of Omagh's most precious glens. From here, it is hard to imagine that atrocities could ever have happened in this part of the world. But if you want to find an ecoescape which represents a bewilderingly peaceful Northern Ireland, this is the place.

Contact details
Address: The Omagh Hostel, 9a Waterworks Road, Omagh, County Tyrone BT79 7JS
Telephone: +44 (0) 28 8224 1973
Website: www.omaghhostel.co.uk
Price: Beds £12.50 per person for a dormitory room and £15 per person sharing a private room. Children under three are free. Camping is £20 per night, per tent. Orienteering, minimum 10 people, £150 for half a day
Opening times: Beginning of March to the end of October

© Lesley Bulman

Disabled access: Good wheelchair facilities, with ground floor accommodation and adapted bathrooms

Getting there slowly
Take the bus to Omagh. Billy or Marella will pick you up if necessary. The hostel is five kilometres from the bus station. Omagh is on the Sustrans cycle route 92 (www.sustrans.org).

Eat at Chez Manu
In Omagh town centre, Chez Manu is a small locally-run café, with great coffee and generous sandwiches, but best known as the crepes 'meisters' of Omagh. En route home from a hike, you'll get a good welcome at McGinns pub in Killyclogher, a 30-minute walk from the Omagh Hostel.
Address: Chez Manu, 76a Market Square, Omagh, County Tyrone BT79 0AA
Telephone: +44 (0) 28 8225 2528

the West

The West

"At Gregans Castle Hotel, we strive to minimise our footprint on the environment", says the welcome pack in the Galway Bay Suite. It is not hard to see why, when you look out the window onto one of the most unique landscapes in Ireland. This is the Burren, one of Ireland's most celebrated National Parks. Simon and Frederieke, the owners, are aware of the privileged position they hold high up in a valley of this extraordinary limestone landscape. The interior design of each room or suite is individual, yet always majestic. The colours seem to be inspired by the view beyond each window. Purple greys for the heathers, lichen greens, creamy whites and pinks for the alpine flowers and soft greys for the flat stones spreading out for miles around them. It is fitting, therefore, that the majority of paints used are natural.

Simon and Fred do not play Lord and Lady of the manor, which many might be tempted to, as owners of such an exquisite house. They are leaders in the community, taking a strong stance on sustaining the Burren, as well as the livelihoods of those who live there – most importantly the farmers. The hotel is a member of the Burren Beef and Lamb Producers Group and has committed to sourcing all such meat locally. Likewise, the chef buys all the smoked fish, salads, eggs and cheeses from small Burren producers.

It is also one of the first luxury hotels of this standard in Ireland to pursue the EU Flower accreditation. They have started with a natural peat moss water treatment plant, cleaned by coppiced Scarlet Willow. There is a wood pellet boiler in the staff accommodation, with another one for guests planned in 2009. Eight bicycles are available for visitors, and their neighbour, a local guide, archaeologist, local historian and farmer, gives daily walking tours across the Burren.

t: +353 (0) 65 707 7005
w: www.gregans.ie

These are not just grand gestures from the grand house. It has been the family's ethos since they opened. That is why there are no tellies in the rooms, "for uninterrupted views of the stunning landscape". Thank goodness, they are doing their bit to protect it.

Contact details

Address: Gregans Castle Hotel, Ballyvaughan, County Clare
Telephone: +353 (0) 65 707 7005
Website: www.gregans.ie
Price: Rooms and suites from €190 to €450 per person sharing, including breakfast. There are reduced rates for single occupancy
Opening times: Open Thursday to Sunday, February and March and then open every day until end of November. Closed December and January
Disabled access: There are no steps up to the hotel. Several rooms are on the ground floor, with direct access onto gardens, and two bedrooms have low baths

Getting there slowly

Take the train or bus to Galway, then there's a choice of two buses, one to Ballyvaughan village (5km from Gregans), or the Galway to Doolin bus which passes the front gate of Gregans. There are two of these a day, and one in winter.

Visit the Burren Perfumery

Take a free tour of the Perfumery's plant-based still and organic herb garden with culinary, medicinal and cosmetic herbs on show. This place is an aromatic arena of simple beauty. There is an audiovisual slideshow about the Burren and its flora, after which you can tuck into many of the Perfumery's fine organic cuisine in its tea rooms. Herbal tea is, of course, a must. The tea rooms are open daily from March until September, and at weekends in April.
Address: The Burren Perfumery, Carron, County Clare
Telephone: +353 (0) 65 708 9102
Website: www.burrenperfumery.com

This visitor centre was, and still is, controversial. It took fifteen years to build and cost €31 million. Ireland is falling down with 'interpretive centres', many of which do little to interpret, and receive a paltry number of visitors. However, this is not an interpretive centre. Nor is it an expensive marketing exercise. It is a guardian of one of Ireland's most treasured landscapes, the mighty Cliffs of Moher. A veritable coup de theatre, this stunning architectural creation is a most fitting gesture for such a dramatic and awe-inspiring piece of Ireland's natural heritage.

I was so excited to see this building which cost a fortune, had coach-drivers banging on their horns at increased car park fees, and local landowners stomping their feet over access, that I forgot one important thing when I arrived. You can't actually see it. It is subterranean, set into the hill, with a living grass lid over the whole thing. The grass seed for this part of the process was taken to be harvested from the site, before building even began. The architects had sustainability and concealment at the top of their priority list. There is a state-of-the-art geo-thermal heating and cooling system built into the hill, solar panels which provide 75% of hot water needs, and an on-site water treatment plant, which includes a grey water recycling system for use in toilets and irrigating the living roof. The designers are certainly not shouting about their achievements from the clifftops. All the good things are hidden from view, and yet it succeeds in treading extremely lightly on land which is visited by almost a million tourists a year.

Inside the cave-like structure, there are informative exhibitions, aptly called Atlantic Edge, and a virtual reality experience, called 'The Ledge', which is

t: +353 (0) 65 708 6140
w: www.cliffsofmoher.ie

a CGI film about the area's sealife above and below sea level. It saves you hanging over the edge of the real thing to try and spot some, which some people still try to do. Such people are now in a minority thanks to newly-appointed well-informed rangers, impressive barriers, fronted with local Liscannor stone slabs, and underpinned walkways to protect the visitors from dangers of landslides. These developments serve only to highlight, not undermine, the beauty of the place for visitors.

I chose to visit the Centre first, walking around the exhibitions, feeding the children in the café, going to the toilet, before heading for the Cliffs themselves. It seemed apt that they should take the final curtain call of the day. Whatever order you choose, do visit and support the exhibitions. Paying the car park fee will help pay the wages of the people who are employed here. But by paying the extra small contribution to see the exhibitions, you will not only learn more about the Cliffs and the region, you will also be ensuring that this non-profit making organisation will survive to keep this special place in the good protective hands into which it has been lucky enough to fall.

Contact details
Address: Cliffs of Moher Visitor Experience, Cliffs of Moher, County Clare
Telephone: +353 (0) 65 708 6140
Website: www.cliffsofmoher.ie
Price: Car Park €8, Atlantic Edge exhibitions Adults €4, Children (4-16) €2.50, Student/ Seniors €3.50, Children under 4 free. Family package (two adults and four children) €11.95
Opening times: Year round (see website or telephone for exact times)
Disabled access: Excellent facilities, with specially-designed ramps at the cliffs as part of walkways and wheelchair access throughout the new building

Getting there slowly
There is a summer bus service, the number 337, from Limerick to the coach park at the Cliffs of Moher. Or take a bus from Galway to Ballyvaughan where you can hire a bike at Burren Bike, which is ideal for discovering the Burren and the Cliffs (visit www.burrenbike.com or telephone +353 (0) 65 707 7061).

A white Connemara pony greeted us upon arrival at Cnoc Suain, high up in the peat boglands overlooking Spiddal's coastline, 22 km from Galway. Neptune, the family pony, stood casually outside the white-washed thatched cottage, in this aptly named Cnoc Suain, meaning 'the restful hill', as if posing for a clichéd, out-dated picture postcard. But there is nothing clichéd or outdated here. Cnoc Suain, overlooking its own Cnoch a Loch, is in its own league of uniqueness, charm and beauty.

Yet Charlie and Dearbhaill, the owners, are still searching for the right name to describe Cnoc Suain. Cultural village, hub, community all reek of cultural com-mercialisation to me. In contrast, this is a family homestead, which they have preserved, rebuilt and opened up to guests. They wanted visitors to stop and absorb culture from this Irish-speaking region of Ireland, rather than glimpsing it through a coach window. They have almost single-handedly rebuilt and thatched four dry-stone wall cottages, installed geothermal underfloor heating, and furnished them in a traditional, simple, and comfortable way.

t: +353 (0) 91 555 703
w: www.cnocsuain.com

On Wednesday and Saturday nights, performers (including Dearbhaill, a professional musician), gather in the main house, in front of the biggest log fire I have ever seen. This feels like friends gathering to perform their traditional 'noble call', be it playing the pipes, sean-nós dancing and singing, or reciting a Yeats poem. Just to make sure you don't feel the cold en route back down the lane to your cottage afterwards, you can stop for a hot whisky at Cnoc Suain's own 'shebeen', where, if you're lucky, the singing goes on until the early hours. Charlie and Dearbhaill are committed conservationists, and are in the process of creating a field laboratory, using microscopes to study elements of the local ecosystem, which includes seashore, bog and Karst limestone. They have also opened up Charlie's extensive library to visitors. There are several options for staying at Cnoc Suain. You can sign up for a weekend residential course in anything from Irish herbal cures to watercolour painting, or if you are in the area, take part in a half-day course. You can also use the cottages as self-catering accommodation, and just lap up the landscape, live and breathe the Gaeltacht culture, and enjoy the open-house feel of Charlie and Dearbhaill's homestead. One request is that children should be over fifteen because bogholes can be dangerous for younger children.

Sustaining local culture is a vital part of developing a responsible tourism business. What makes this place unique is that it is not preserving Irish language, music, cookery and crafts in order to enshrine them. Charlie and Dearbhaill are keeping them alive, contemporising them. This is no theme park. There is nothing tacky or commercial here. It is a place of living culture, oozing with pride and determination to protect and share some of the joys of its heritage.

Contact details
Address: Cnoc Suain, Spiddal, County Galway
Telephone: +353 (0) 91 555 703
Website: www.cnocsuain.com
Price: Residential weekends from €450 and self-catering from €500 per week
Opening times: November-February
Disabled access: Wheelchair access is limited at present, but there are plans for improvement

Getting there slowly
Board the train to Galway, and from there take a taxi or bus to Spiddal and walk – it's only five kilometres on the road passing through blanket bogland.

Visit Brigit's Garden
Spend the day at the stunning Brigit's Garden in nearby Roscahill. There are four gardens created and landscaped to represent the four seasons according to Celtic mythology and tradition of festivals: Samhain, Imbolc, Bealtaine and Lughnasa. This is a place of serenity, spirituality and beauty, where each sculpture, shrub and shrine has been carefully created and installed to represent different aspects of ancient wisdom. Their superb café mirrors the general spiritual ethos of stillness, with a slow (and fine) food policy.
Address: Brigit's Garden, Pollagh, Roscahill, County Galway
Telephone: +353 (0) 91 550 905
Website: www.brigitsgarden.ie

I can't think of a better way of escaping the roar of the Celtic Tiger. This is Irish family hospitality at its finest and most traditional. The owners of these three converted farm outhouses are Niall and Inez Heenan, the fourth generation to live on this 150-acre farm in Terryglass.

Tír na Fiúise is perfect for families. There are three clean and spacious traditional cottages with cupboards full of games, a shed full of bikes, hurling sticks, tennis rackets and a specially made wall to bash a ball against. The cottages are extensions of the Heenan family farm, with pieces of refurbished antique family furniture in many of the rooms. Niall gave me his perfect definition of sustainable tourism. "It keeps us here on our farm in real rural Ireland – I hope it will also be something for our children to inherit and make their own". Committed to rural and environmental conservation, everything is recycled at the farm, and Niall assures me that energy consumption on the sauna is lower than making a few cups of tea.

There are also two new one-bedroom apartments on another part of the farm, built to look like authentic cottages. Ingeniously, these apartments have adjoining doors, so that you can rent both units if required. Good for keeping in-laws or teenagers at arm's length.

You can cycle or walk into Terryglass village, which is almost chocolate box in its quaintness. Situated on Lough Derg, it plays host to boat holidaymakers in summer, but is the perfect small community all year round. Catch this at its best during the Terrryglass Arts Festival, at the end of August. Reservations are

t: +353 (0) 67 22 041
w: www.countrycottages.ie

from Saturday to Saturday, so you can stop at the Nenagh Farmers' market and stock up for the week. Or cycle into Borrisokane for local supplies. For longer trips, you can join up with the Lough Derg and Shannon Region Cycleway.

A journalist once asked Niall, "Why do people come to Terryglass? There is nothing here." Niall's answer was that it is for people who are in search of nothing. For them, the place is enough. Walk the bog at sunrise, and you will understand what he means.

Contact details
Address: Tír na Fiúise, Terryglass, Borrisokane, North Tipperary
Telephone: +353 (0) 67 22 041
Website: www.countrycottages.ie
Price: One bedroom cottage from €200-400 per week, two bedroom cottage from €400-580 per week
Opening times: All year round. Weekend bookings taken in low season only
Disabled access: New one bedroom apartments built to accommodate wheelchair users

Getting there slowly
Take the train to Limerick and then the bus to Nenagh, 30km from Terryglass by taxi. Or bus to Portumna, only 8km from Terryglass. There is also a daily bus to Borrisokane (12km from Terryglass). Niall and Inez can arrange pick up by local taxi.

Drink at Paddy's and eat at the Derg Inn
Take a sup in the wood panelled snug at Paddy's by the peat fire. Stools are made out of beer barrels and the volume on the obligatory television is kept down low. The bar food is good, but pop next door to the Derg Inn for top cuisine. They use local and organic ingredients whenever possible, guaranteeing the use of Irish meat. The beefburger and chips went down brilliantly in our camp, especially the children. Booking is recommended in high season.
Address: The Derg Inn, Terryglass, Nenagh, North Tipperary (Paddy's Bar is next door)
Telephone: +353 (0) 67 22 037
Website: www.derginn.ie

Connemara teased my senses. The barren landscape, with its shades of brown grasses and scatterings of old stone walls, looked as if it was teetering on the edge of death when, bang, suddenly there was a splash of green on the mountains and yellow gorses in a field, and it jumped back to life again. The 18th Century Ballynahinch Castle is right in the heart of this roller coaster trip on the eye.

Inside, the portraits and landscapes paint Ballynahinch's rich history, while Patrick O'Flaherty, the General Manager, delighted in telling me tales of his ancestors. The shelves of the Thomas Martin library also retell the story of the Castle and its surrounds. Take the famous Ballynahinch resident and infamous Pirate Queen, Grace O'Malley, who married into the clan. Or the builder of this fine abode, Richard Martin (Humanity Dick), who founded the Society of the Prevention of Cruelty to Animals in the 1800s. It was good to see his portrait over one of the great roaring fireplaces, rather than a hunting trophy.

Today, however, the heart of the Castle is the Ballynahinch River and Lake, and Patrick talked passionately of their continuing efforts to conserve fish stocks. He has fought hard against fish farming and drift nets and, so far, is winning the battle, with salmon stocks doubling since the closure of the Irish drift net fishery in 2007. Regeneration is a theme at Ballynahinch. One thousand Oak trees have been planted recently, and visitors who want to contribute to this

t: +353 (0) 95 31006
w: www.ballynahinch-castle.com

scheme are given a certificate with the GPS coordinates of their own tree, so that they can locate it in years to come. The majority of the hotel's hot water and heating is generated from solar panels and wood-pellet burners, and they recycle as much as possible. You can also eat at the Castle's own Fisherman's Pub or Owenmore restaurant. The same chef prepares the food for both spots, where the words homemade, organic and local feature heavily on the menu.

If the Armada bedroom is free, book that one for the views. It is on a corner, so you really get your money's worth, with views of the Twelve Bens Mountains on one side and the river on the other. But the river was where I was drawn to where, in April, the brown trout were starting to break the water of the lake: Connemara springing to life again.

Contact details
Address: Ballynahinch Castle, Recess, Connemara, County Galway
Telephone: +353 (0) 95 31006
Website: www.ballynahinch-castle.com
Price: €120-240 per person sharing, depending on season. Includes full Irish Breakfast
Opening Times: All year
Disabled access: Good access. No steps up to ground floor, with bedrooms on ground floor

Getting there slowly
Take the bus or train to Galway and then a one-hour Citylink bus trip to Clifden getting off at Canal Bridge. The hotel can pick you up from the bus stop.

Visit the Inisbofin Island
Take a boat from Cleggan, 11km from Clifden, to the island of Inisbofin. The island is a breeding ground for rare Corncrakes and two seal colonies can also be found, one near Stags Rock and the other on the island of Inishgort, just west of Inishbofin Harbour. The latter is only accessible by boat. This island has been inhabited for over six thousand years, and a visit to the Heritage Centre is recommended to get to know the island better. Before heading back, treat yourself to some crab or lobster at one of the island's hotels. Take your swimsuit. The clear water and white sands are irresistable. See www.inishbofin.com and www.irelandsislands.com for details.

Delphi might be a motor-free adventure centre, but the manager and co-owner, Rory Concannon, is firing on all cylinders. He has rescued this treasure of a wood and stone building in the Delphi Valley from receivership, and has spent the last two years revamping it to precise eco standards. The location is an 'ecoescape-extraordinaire', nestled between two contrasting stretches of water: Killary Harbour and the Bundorragha River, which is fed by numerous mountain streams. The rest of Delphi's land is made up of 300 acres of forest, and so it came as a relief to see that the architects have created a suitable sustainable tribute to this picturebook County Galway landscape.

The emphasis is more well-being than spa at Delphi. Some of the many activities on offer include kayaking, cycling, archery, hill-walking, surfing, rock-climbing and raft-building. All carbon neutral. "How sexy is that?" said Rory. Personally, I found the idea of collapsing in my luxurious maisonette suite more appealing, with French windows opening out onto the mountains and logs burning in the wooden stove. I could hear nothing but the river rushing past us into the bay. Even 'sexier', not a whine or a whimper from our children, who had been whisked off to take part in archery and kayaking sessions.

There is one more inspired touch at Delphi. The chef, Gerard Reidy thrives on the availability of fresh food growing, swimming and grazing on his doorstep. Fresh mussels from their own Killary Bay, and Connemara lamb were two such fine courses on the menu when I visited. Environmentally they are way

t: +353 (0) 95 42208
w: www.delphimountainresort.com

ahead of the game. They have installed their own water treatment plant on site, recycle everything, compost, and run all heating and hot water off two wood-energy boilers, (currently wood pellets, but from next year to be sourced from their own managed forests). Insulation is with recycled paper, all water is sourced from the mountain spring, and the roof is made of recycled copper and cedar tiles. So, all revamped and ready to go, Rory has achieved his dream. This place is a beacon of sustainability. And sexiness.

Contact details
Address: Delphi Mountain Resort, Leenane, Connemara, County Galway
Telephone: +353 (0) 95 42208
Website: www.delphimountainresort.com
Price: From €40 per night for a dorm room with breakfast, to €300 for two bedroom, five star suite with breakfast
Opening times: All year round
Disabled access: Excellent facilities for wheelchair users including lift

Getting there slowly
Take a train to Westport, and Delphi will arrange station transfers. There is also a summer bus service from Galway to Leenane.

Drink at Gaynors and Hamiltons pubs
Both pubs in Leenane are great, although Gaynors is more touristy, as it was the main setting of the famous film 'The Field', which was shot in the town. If you want to sample some of the fine fare fished out of Leenane fjord, try the Blackberry Café, where seafood chowders, mussels and home-made bread are the norm. Open 12-4.30pm and 6-9pm daily in high season.

People like to escape in different ways. Some to the mountains, others to a remote beach. I have a thing about islands, and a particular thing about this one. It draws me back, again and again, and one of these days I will just miss the boat and stay. Like Ciara Cullen, who moved there twenty years ago. If it is a real retreat you are after, her wooden house and cottage in the hills of Clare Island, overlooking the Atlantic, is about as far from the world as you can get.

The Centre is family-run, offers weekend and week-long yoga breaks, as well as courses in vegetarian cooking and eco-building. As experts in both, you can assume that the food is great, and the building is top notch eco. Ciara and her husband Christophe have created the textbook ecoescape. Accommodation is in a restored traditional island cottage, with workshops in the new wooden building, both fusing organically with the island's rugged landscape. There are solar panels for heating water, wood-burning stoves, as well as the use of natural materials such as wood, hemp and lime plaster, terracotta and natural slates. They grow and source as many of their ingredients as locally as possible on the island, although the gusty, and often ghastly, weather can be prohibitive. There are no water shortages, however, as they have their own well.

The Centre is set on 240 acres of mainly mountain land grazed by sheep and horses, as well as ten acres of native woodland. Every year, they set aside an area of land for tree planting and, in the past four years, have planted more than 5,000 trees. Purist, yes. Precious, absolutely not. Clare Island just isn't

t: +353 (0) 98 25 412
w: www.yogaretreats.ie

like that. It is rare to come away without mucky wellies, messed up hair and sand just about everywhere. Not to mention the often bumpy boat trip, which puts the 'green' into your break quicker than you might have thought. But, when I step off the boat, walk across the island's small strand, stroll up the lighthouse road to Ciara's house meeting hardly anyone except the sheep and horses on the way, my heart, soul and stomach are on the mend within minutes.

Contact details
Address: Clare Island Yoga Retreat Centre, The Healing Path, Ballytoughey, Clare Island, County Mayo
Telephone: +353 (0) 98 25 412
Website: www.yogaretreats.ie
Price: Retreats range from €250 to €1,100 depending on the course. 'Open house' available when courses are not running for visitors looking for accommodation, food and a yoga session. Price is €90 a day, for three days' minimum stay
Opening times: All year round
Disabled access: None

Getting there slowly
Take the bus or train to Westport, and then taxi to Roonagh Pier. For taxi contact Michael O'Hare, +353 (0) 87 220 2123 and say you are staying at the Centre. You cannot take your car to the Island, but bike hire is available at the island's quay.

Visit the Ballytoughey Loom
The Ballytoughey Loom is where Beth Moran, a weaver and master craftswoman, has set up her own loom and crafts shop. If you want the best excuse to stay on the island for even longer, you can take part in one of Beth's weekend or week-long workshops in spinning, weaving and natural dying.
Address: Ballytoughey Loom, Clare Island, County Mayo
Telephone: +353 (0) 98 25800
Website: www.clareisland.info/loom

Enniscoe will always make me think of eiderdowns. "Can't find anyone to mend them these days. It's such a shame, I would hate to lose them," said Susan Kellett who, as one of the villagers described her is "the lovely lady at the big pink house on the lake". Susan maintains her Georgian manor house, with an eiderdown ethos. They are on the beds, because that was what was always there. There is no central heating, and yet even in mid-February, I never felt a shiver with its roaring fires and night-time storage heating. The fire in my bedroom was lit when I arrived, casting shadows over the four-poster bed, and accompanying nursery bed for my son.

Susan wears plenty of layers, and isn't afraid to get her fingernails dirty in the vegetable garden. This no-nonsense approach is echoed throughout Enniscoe. There is a feeling of faded glamour, but without a hint of shabbiness. One of the most quirky features is the eclectic art collection, dominated by Susan's mother's work. I could have spent a whole day just looking at her paintings, each with a story to tell.

t: +353 (0) 96 31112
w: www.enniscoe.com

Susan's attitude to sustainability comes from generations of 'close the door and keep the heat in' attitudes, characteristic of many grand house owners, for whom 'being green' was practical, long before it was politically correct. The wetland waste water system goes back to 1800, there is a stunning three-acre walled monumental garden, an organic vegetable garden and orchard, used not only by Susan, but also by the local community, and water is sourced from their well. The recently redecorated spiral stairwell was done with limewater plaster because, "you can't put new on old. It just doesn't work".

Susan is so lacking in pretensions that she almost undersells Enniscoe. As I took my walk around Lough Conn, accompanied by Frodo, Susan's faithful Labrador, and looked back along the long, wooded path to the house, I noticed that the main entrance looks out over the lake, rather than to visitors approaching up the long tree-lined driveway. It is almost as if the focus was always intended to be on the view, rather than on how they were viewed. Just as it should be and, for what it's worth, this visitor was totally enthralled.

Contact details
Address: Enniscoe House, Castlehill, Ballina, County Mayo
Telephone: +353 (0) 96 31112
Website: www.enniscoe.com
Price: Bed and breakfast prices, per person sharing, range from €90-116 per night. Courtyard apartments between €450 and €800 per week

Opening times: Self-catering open all year, main house open April-November
Disabled access: There are three courtyard apartments, one of which has been designed to accommodate wheelchair users

Getting there slowly
Bus or train to Ballina, and then take a fifteen-minute taxi journey. Susan can also arrange bike hire for visitors.

Visit the Foxford Woollen Mills Visitor Centre
Take a break from boating and fishing on Lough Conn to stock up your woollen and tweeds from one of Ireland's oldest and most famous mills at Foxford. The Foxford Woollen Mills Visitor Centre is a recently refurbished museum which shows how the town grew up around the mill since it was set up in 1892. However, it is still a working mill and you can take a tour of the weaving, dyeing and finishing operations, then move onto the shop, with its impressive array of tweed designs. There are great lunches in the restaurant and if you are there on a Saturday morning you can catch the farmers' market in the courtyard.
Address: Foxford Woollen Mills Visitor Centre, Foxford, County Mayo
Telephone: +353 (0) 94 925 6756
Website: www.museumsofmayo.com

If you are booking a self-catering place with a Saturday to Saturday stay, which is often the norm, it is worth getting on the road a couple of hours early just to stop at the farmers' market on the way, and stock up for the week.

My favourite experience of this was arriving into Belfast off the ferry at dawn, on an icy Saturday winter morning. I found my way to the sleepy, city centre and fell upon St. George's Market. The City Food and Garden Market takes place from 9am until 3pm, but I was there at 8am, and there were plenty of stall holders happy to sell at that time. Cakes from "Wee Buns" and Fairtrade organic coffee were a great start to the day. Other stalls include fish from Portavogie, pork from Cookstown, beef from Armagh, cheese from Leitrim, pheasant in season and several stalls of organic vegetables. When the jazz band started up a bit later, I realised that my morning was lost, but so much else was gained. There is

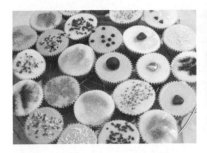

no better way of starting a journey than this. The beloved and much-needed food suppliers are what keep a country alive, after all.

The traditional market at St George's is the Variety Market on a Friday. Dating back to 1604, this is open from 6am until 1pm, with nearly 250 stalls, selling everything from salmon to slippers. The market is a quick walk from Central train station, but there is a free market shuttle-bus (from 8am) to and from the market, every 30 minutes. Pick-up points include Botanic station, Castle Court Centre on Royal Avenue, and from the Park and Ride on York Street (from 8am Fridays and 9am Saturdays). On a Thursday, there is also a farmers' market at the Park Centre, Donegal Road in West Belfast, between 10am and 5pm.

If you want to experience this great way to start your ecoescape at other ports of call in Ireland, check out the Dublin Docklands Farmers Market, Excise Walk, International Financial Services Centre, Dublin, (Thursdays from 10am-3pm). You can walk straight off the ferry at Dublin port and up the quays to this one. The Farmers' Market in Temple Bar's Meeting House Square, Saturdays 9am-5pm and Wednesday 11am-3pm, is a popular Dublin place to hang out, with about thirty stalls selling Irish chocolates, cheeses, and sausages to name but a few. If you

are coming into Dun Laoghaire port, you are spoilt for choice. On a Thursday, you can pop into Dun Laoghaire Shopping Centre Market, between 10am-5pm, or there is one in the harbour itself on a Saturday, at the Dun Laoghaire Harbour Yacht club, between 10am-4pm. Or if you are taking a Sunday afternoon stroll down the pier, go via the People's Park, where there is a market between 11am-4pm. The nearest big market to Rosslare is in Wexford, on a Friday, between 9am-2pm (see www.wexfordfarmersmarket.com). In Cork, the ferry might no longer be functioning, but the market is one of the busiest and buzziest in Ireland. Known as The English Market, and dating back to 1610, this covered market is daily, a gourmand's heaven, particularly if you love fish. Great coffee shops here too.

There are approximately 130 farmers' markets in Ireland, and the list is growing all the time. There is not enough room here to highlight all of them, but as well as the ones mentioned above, some of the leading ones are as follows:

Athlone, Saturday 10am-3pm, Market Square

Boyle, Saturday 10am-2pm, Kings House

Cahir, Saturday 9am-1pm, beside The Craft Granary

Carrick-on-Shannon, Thursday 10am-2pm, Market Yard

Dingle, Friday 10am-4pm, opposite the harbour

Ennis, Friday 8am-2pm, Upper Market St Car Park

Galway, Saturday 9am-5pm, Sunday 2pm-6pm, beside St. Nicholas' church

Kilkenny, third Sunday in month 10am-2pm, Gowran Community Hall

Kinsale, Tuesday 9.30am-1.30pm, Short Quay

Limerick, Saturday 8am-2pm, Milk Market Building

Newry, Friday 9am-2pm, Marketplace

Skibbereen, Saturday 9.30am-1.30pm, Old Market Square

Sligo, Saturday 9am-1pm, Sligo Institute of Technology

Tralee, Friday 9am-5pm

Waterford, Saturday 10am-4pm, Jenkins Lane

Market times sometimes change, due to closure, season or merging with other markets. For the quickest reference to times and locations, see www.irelandmarkets.com. Other good sources of information on food festivals and artisans can be found at www.westernorganicnetwork.com and www.slowfoodireland.com.

One thing that will strike any visitors to Ireland, especially if they are out and about in the early evening, is the number of walkers. Not just people walking their dogs, but fit, speedy walkers who look as if they are in training for the Olympic walking race. In Dublin, for example, you will see teams of trainer-clad office workers striding home at the end of the day.

Walking is, in fact, the number one leisure activity in Ireland and there are end-less stunning landscapes to try out your fitness levels. Waymarked Ways of Ireland manages an impressive and ever-growing network of walks in Ireland. This serves many purposes. Environmentally, it protects the land from over-trampling, and socially, it centralises the solving of land access issues which are so prevalent in Ireland. Finally, economically, the Waymarked Ways aims to entice more visitors back to rural Ireland again. The Irish might be donning their boots, but visitors are still leaving theirs at home, favouring bar stools in Dublin over those in a village in the Bluestack Mountains.

At present, there are 31 Waymarked Ways around Ireland, covering almost 3,000 kilometres. Many of these are hundreds of kilometres long, but the website and accompanying maps divide them into different sections, giving guidance on lev-els of difficulty on each walk. You can also order, or download, a copy of the organisation's "Selected Day Walks" leaflet for shorter strolls. The website

t: +353 (0) 18 60 8800
w:www.walkireland.ie

is user-friendly, with interactive maps and a search engine, so you can just put in an area or town, and find your nearest way to walk there. They have up to date news on Ireland's many walking festivals, rambling clubs and general walking news, such as the annual Cuckoo Walking Festival in County Kerry in May, or Anascaul & Inch Walking Festival in October.

This website does not cover Northern Ireland. The Countryside Access & Activities Network for Northern Ireland (CAAN) runs an extremely informative website, www.walkni.com. This also has detailed user-friendly maps and one excellent additional feature of this website is the "getting to and from the walk" section. You will find this under "Useful info", and it gives public transport options for accessing one of their trails. One other excellent website for walkers is www.coilteoutdoors.ie, run by Ireland's forestry commission. There is a plethora of information on cycling and walking trails throughout Ireland's forest parks.

Visitors will get to benefit from the growing Irish trend for walking, as the Irish government is increasing its role in supporting the Waymarked Ways. It recently established a National Trails Office under the Department for Arts, Sports and Tourism. Its aim is to develop the existing network into a world-class network of walking, cycling, horseriding and canoeing trails. It has also introduced a new scheme to invite farmers to become more involved with maintenance of walking routes. This is important as most of the land in Ireland is privately owned by farmers, although a recent survey undertaken by Teagasc, the Irish Agricultural and Food Development Authority, showed that 50% of farmers were still unwilling to participate in walking schemes. Clearly, this is still delicate territory, and it is good to see that these issues are being discussed at government level.

This continued proactive and forward-thinking management of Ireland's trails also offers great scope for the development of local businesses along the way, such as accommodation, cafés, restaurants, bicycle and canoe hire, many of which already feature in ecoescape. So, once you discover the series of trails which cover the varied Irish landscape of rugged coasts, lakelands, mountains and blanket bog, the internationally renowned pub trails may just start to pale into insignificance. Or provide the perfect hangover cure, of course.

Telephone: +353 (0) 18 60 8800
Website: www.walkireland.ie

The ecoescape slow travel toolkit

ecoescape is all about travelling slowly

When we discover new ecoescapes, we like to travel slowly. We try to avoid airports and motorways and have spent days, perhaps weeks travelling by trains and buses. This has brought its own adventures. Like when we've missed a connection, for example, the added time in a place is more time to get to know it. When we've been on the train we've chatted to people or simply admired the view from the window.

So in this section of the guide, we've put together a useful toolkit to help you to find slow ways to travel to and around Ireland, many of which we've tried out ourselves. There are also ideas for places to stay and visit that all try in many ways to reduce their impact on the environment.

So what is Slow all about?

The Slow Food Movement began in 1989 and is now filtering into many aspects of our modern lifestyles. Carlo Petrini established the world famous Slow Food Movement in defiance of mass-produced fast food which was having an increasingly damaging impact on health and the environment. The Movement is about exploring regional flavours and well-loved ingredients as well as spending mealtimes sharing food with other people in our lives.

Like the Slow Food Movement, slow travel celebrates regional diversity but in the context of journeys and holidays. Rather than arriving at our destinations as quickly as possible, slow travellers use the journey as an opportunity to get to know the places and people they meet along the way. So this means that sharing journeys is as impor-

tant to slow travel as mealtimes are for slow food. This can only be achieved by taking the train or bus or other form of public transport. Like slow food, slow travel has less impact on the environment. It involves forms of transport like cycling and walking that have low or no carbon emissions. ■

Slow travel in Ireland

"You must be afraid of flying, are you?" is the question from every taxi driver dropping me to the ferry in Dublin Port en route to London. I explain that I prefer to travel that way, when possible, because I've had enough of airports and air travel. It is hard to get a Dublin taxi driver to stop talking, but this one usually gets them every time. They look at me in their rear view mirror like I have two heads. I am afraid of flying, of course, but not through any phobia. The biggest problem with air travel is climate change. Its relative contribution in worldwide carbon emissions is still low, but it is one of the fastest growing sources of climate changing gases. If, according to Friends of the Earth, air travel grows at its current rate it will become the biggest source of carbon dioxide pollution by 2040. The skies are opening up more and more all the time, and governments are doing little to stop it. People are being encouraged to reduce their energy consumption at home and on the road, but everywhere you turn there is an advert for cheap flights. But I usually spare the taxi driver all of this, and just tell them the other truth. I like travelling slowly. It's better for my head.

Slow travel is a huge issue in Ireland because, of course, it is an island. They need and welcome tourists, and most of them want to fly there. One Irish man's bid to take over the skies continues, as the Celtic Harp emblazoned on his world-famous budget airline soars from city to city, like some sort of conquering warrior besporting blue and yellow warpaint. Budget flights may be helping tourist boards hit their targets, but they are creating a different type of tourism. In Ireland, this is mainly urban, giving the cities a chance to show that they can keep up with the cosmopolitan competition around the globe.

Meanwhile, visitors to Ireland, and Irish people themselves, are ignoring the vast majority of the country: rural Ireland. They are forgetting to slow down and just get out of town. Jetting around is very much in the Celtic zeitgeist at the moment. According to a recent National Irish Bank survey, entitled "The Emerald Isle – The Wealth of Modern Ireland", the Irish are buying more luxury private jets than anywhere else in Europe. They are not letting the green grass grow under their feet anymore. Out with the clichéd images of men smoking pipes on donkeys. Ireland's recent economic growth has brought Ireland into the twenty first century flying its flag proudly on the world map of commercial achievements. Consequently, car ownership is at an all time high, and one hotel I visited

recently had "Visit our local car showroom", on its list of things to do nearby. The cars are newer and faster, and so are the roads, which may explain why the State still has one of the highest rate of road accidents in Europe.

As the economy begins to take that necessary slowing down pill, so tourists might follow suit. We Irish used to make fun of American tourists who did the Ring of Kerry in the morning, Hill of Tara in the afternoon, and then fit in a bit of O'Casey at The Abbey Theatre that night, only to jump on a plane and do London the next day. Now, many Irish people don't even think twice about a weekend's shopping in New York, or a weekend escape to play golf in the Gulf.

As I live in London, I have taken the slow route to Ireland numerous times during the research period for this book. I have tried and tested just about every route, ferry service, train and coach service. I now look forward to my trips, taking time out to read, write, listen to music, and breathe in the landscapes of three countries in one day. It has changed the way I think about travel, although that is not to say it is always the easy option. I have missed connections, been sick on the boat, and had ferries cancelled at short notice. But on the upside, I have had no luggage restrictions, no queues, friendly service, and done a day's work en route.

I confess that I did not research the book entirely by slow travel, but I did my best. Out of all my research trips, I flew only once, to Knock airport, as the logistics of getting from England to the West of Ireland at that time were proving impossible. I hired a car to get around, or else it was going to take a year to research the book. I would have loved that luxury, but it would have been out of date by the time I had finished the research. This is taking the realistic approach, which is what most travellers have to do, even if they are trying to change their travel habits. I have provided slow travel options to every featured ecoescape, and even though it was impossible for me to take these modes of transport every time, I took trains, buses, canoes and bikes, whenever I could. Environmental purists will disagree, but if we all reduced our flights to one in ten journeys in or out of Ireland, and left the car at home for weekend breaks, the statistics would soon start to change.

Louis L'Amour, the US novelist, said, "The trail is the thing, not the end of the trail. Travel too fast and you miss all you are travelling for". The best way to do this in Ireland is, of course, to walk. It is one of the most popular leisure activities in the country, and most definitely the slowest. There is a superb network of walking trails (see Waymarked Ways of Ireland on pages 149-150), all of which took me into an Ireland which I thought was disappearing. So, if you thought it was becoming a concrete and tarmac jungle out there too, get your boots on and your map out. The mountains, lakes, rivers and islands are all there for visiting, and there are many people out there who have set up extraordinary sustainable tourism businesses, just waiting to open their doors to you. ■ **CM**

Getting to and around Ireland slowly

Taking the ferry

There are several ferry options for travelling to and from Ireland. You can get a fast ferry or slow ferry, travel by foot or as a car passenger, to Dublin, Dun Laoghaire, Belfast, or Rosslare. Some services do not allow you to travel as a foot passenger but when they do, you can carry liquids, pushchairs, wheelchairs, bicycles, a surfboard, musical instruments – hopefully you get the picture. Most ferry companies tie in with SailRail (see below), an alliance which offers excellent deals when combining the train from several UK stations to Ireland, such as £27 single for London to Dublin, rail and ferry. For details of any train connections in Ireland, UK or France, see award-winning site www.seat61.com. There is also useful information on accessing ferry ports at www.directferries.co.uk

The carbon emission statistics for ferry travel are still unreliable, and like airlines, so much depends on the age and speed of the vessel, as well as the levels of marine policing and passenger occupancy. Few ferry companies have publicly-available environmental policies, or indeed any visible signs of on-board restrictions such as recycling, energy or water conservation. So, until the scientists can get the statistics, it is left to the traveller to make a choice. Mine is to try and take the boat and train as much as possible, because unless demand for these services increases, I don't believe that governments, tour companies, ferry and rail organisations, will get their act together to improve services and reduce emissions. If we show them we, the consumers, are trying to make a difference, then they might actually lay on a few more trains, recycling bins, bike racks, and generally improved infrastructure to help us on our way.

Irish Ferries

Irish Ferries claims to operate "one of the world's youngest and most fuel efficient ferry fleets", as well as the largest car ferry in the world, the Ulysses. It also has a detailed and publicly available environmental policy. The company claims that CO_2 emissions per passenger/km for travel by ferry are 3-5 times lower than those of travel by air or by car. Indeed, one carbon calculator on a family rail/sail trip to Ireland calculated our total emissions at 0.42 tonnes, compared to 1.31 tonnes for the same journey by rail and air. As a regular passenger, the Ulysses is indeed huge, staff are friendly and helpful and you can nearly always get a seat (I managed to, even on a Friday afternoon travelling from Holyhead on a rugby international weekend between Wales and Ireland). They travel between Ireland and Wales, Dublin-Holyhead, Rosslare to Pembroke, and to France from Rosslare to Cherbourg and Roscoff. Foot passenger single tickets cost from €35 between Ireland and the UK, and from €56 between Ireland and France. If you are travelling by car, there is an additional cost of €15 if you book by telephone, so best to book online.

There are two services between Dublin and Holyhead, North Wales. One on the faster Catamaran, named after the Irish writer, Jonathan Swift, (one hour 49 minutes) and the other, is the slower cruise ferry (three hours 15 minutes), the Ulysses. If you are travelling in peak season, you can upgrade to Club Class where there are more seats available. There are also complimentary snacks of smoked salmon, cheese and biscuits. It's advisable not to depend on the Swift crossing, as it seems to be cancelled in anything other than perfect sailing conditions. Not something the Irish Sea is famous for. But I have always been successfully and automatically transferred to the next Ulysses crossing when this has happened, which is earlier, and so has not affected my train connections.

Between UK and Dublin, you check in your luggage and carry any hand luggage you need. Between Rosslare and Pembroke, foot Pas-

The Ulyssees Ferry, Dublin Port.

sengers are brought from the terminal buildings in to the ship by bus. The bus travels with the ship so you can, if you wish, leave your luggage on the bus. On French routes, you bring your luggage on board with you.

Arriving into Dublin Port is spectacular. We glided past walkers taking an evening stroll along the South Wall, one of my favourite Dublin spots, which separates Dublin Bay from the River Liffey. The Wicklow Mountains dominate the landscape in the background, and the famous Dublin landmark, the red and white chimneys fill the foreground. The captain moored the vast ferry as if it was a Mini. If you want to rent a car, the only company to 'meet and greet' you at Dublin Port is Dan Dooley. Book in advance at www.dan-dooley.ie. Minutes from the town centre, you can catch a bus, if your luggage isn't late, and I have missed it several times. But it is a short taxi ride to city centre, and people often share one for a couple of Euros each. For details of bus times to and from Dublin City Centre to Dublin Port, see www.dublinbus.ie. There are railway stations at Holyhead, Pembroke, Rosslare, Cherbourg and Roscoff so transfers are easy. See www.seat61.com for details.

Website: www.irishferries.com
Telephone: +353 (0) 818 300 400 for Republic of Ireland residents or 08705 17 17 17 for UK residents

Stena Line

Stena Line travels to and from ports in Northern Ireland and Republic of Ireland, with sailings between Holyhead and Dublin port or Dun Laoghaire, Fishguard to Rosslare, Fleetwood to Larne and Stranraer in Scotland to Belfast. The Fleetwood to Larne crossing is the longest, at eight hours, and is not available to foot passengers. Foot passengers between Stranraer and Belfast pay from £23 single.

I took the incredibly fast and smooth Fastcraft from Holyhead to Dun Laoghaire in under two hours. Extremely comfortable, more modern design than some, although with little room up on deck. I was less happy with the outdated public announcement that cigarettes were on sale in the shop, and the constant television noise. The Stena Plus Lounge has complimentary snacks, tea and coffee, as well as desk space and WiFi access.

Stena Lines's environmental policy aims to reduce energy usage by 5% a year, by changing propellers, adjusting time tables and speed analysis. They use lead-free paints on the ship, and they recycle engine heat for heating water and onboard heating, as well as recycle their waste.

There are railway stations at Fishguard, Dun Laoghaire, Stranraer and Rosslare for easy transfers. Dublin's DART trains go directly into the city centre from Dun Laoghaire port.

Website: www.stenaline.co.uk
Telephone: +353 (0) 1 204 7777 for Republic of Ireland residents or 08705 70 70 70 for UK residents

Norfolkline

This is the only overnight crossing I took to Ireland, eight hours from Liverpool to Belfast. Available to foot and car passengers, there is also a day crossing. They offer the same service from Liverpool to Dublin. It was during this journey I realised that most tourist infrastructure was built around airports not ferry ports. You can take a train to Liverpool's ferry port in Birkenhead from the city centre, but it's a fifteen minute walk from the station to the ferry, or a cab ride. A taxi from Liverpool's Lime Street station to Birkenhead port is around £12.

Similarly in Belfast, Norfolkline's ferry port is far from the centre, and taking a taxi is the only option. There is no shuttle bus because, according to Norfolkline, there is no demand. As I was one of five foot passengers, among about fifty truckers that night, I could see why. Make a point of filling in the customer services form in your cabin, lobbying for a shuttle bus. I hired a car from local provider Dan Dooley, again the only company willing to bring one out to the port at 6.30am, although I was charged a supplement for 'anti-social hours'. However, they were very friendly and helpful, just not used to customers arriving by ferry.

The service on board was faultless. The staff bent over backwards to help mothers with pushchairs, and me with my luggage. You can check your luggage in, but remember to pack a separate overnight bag, if you do. Like all ferry terminals, Birkenhead is clean and warm but with basic facilities, snack machines, and the proverbial loud television competing with a noisy video game machine. I was shuttled to the ferry by bus, and onboard, was able to take in Liverpool's night skyline across the Mersey.

It is confusing when you book the ticket online. Cabins are described as four berth, which they are. But if you are travelling alone, you are guaranteed to have the room to yourself. The cabins are clean and roomy, with decent sized beds and crisp cotton bed linen. There is a small desk, giving me the opportunity to catch up on some work. I tried to plug in my laptop, only to find that the plug sockets are for two pin plugs. "It's because it's an Italian boat, Madame." But you can buy a travel plug in the shop.

Norfolkline should consider updating their design from circa 1975 if it wants to sell itself to modern travellers. Vinyl wallpaper, chintzy curtains, and far too much shiny stainless steel around the bars, and the food is so 70s, it is almost kitsch. Fridges with revolving shelves of tinned fruit cocktails, black forest gateaux, paté and crackers, and egg mayonnaise salads. Fricasees and fried fish. As it is included in the price, I felt I must try it and in fairness it was well cooked, just not really my thing.

If you haven't booked a cabin, there is a quiet room, with reclining seats, and blankets for those who want to sleep without the multi-media. I was asleep before we even left Birkenhead, and enjoyed the journey. But there is a market out there for a boutique hotel crossing the Irish Sea. Time to make it feel glamorous again.

Website: www.norfolkline.com
Telephone: +353 (0) 1 819 2999 for Republic of Ireland residents or +44 (0) 8 44 499 0007 for UK residents

P&O Irish Sea

Offering crossings between Scotland and Northern Ireland, as well as one between Dublin and Liverpool, this company does not tie in with SailRail, so you need to book any train travel independently. The services between Larne and Cairnryan or Troon are fast and frequent, and foot passengers travel from £20 for a one-way journey. There is a railway station at Troon, about twenty minute walk from the ferry port. Troon is a 40 minute train journey from Glasgow. If you are travelling to and from Cairnryan, the nearest train station is at Stranraer, about four miles away and taxis are not always available when you need them. It is a half hour cycle around the shore of Lough Ryan and P&O do not charge to transport bikes. There is an hourly train between Larne port and Belfast.

Website: www.poirishsea.com
Telephone: +353 (0) 1 407 34 34 for Republic of Ireland residents or 0871 66 44 999 for UK residents

SailRail

This alliance of train and ferry operators in Ireland and the UK, offers an invaluable service in combining rail and ferry tickets from several UK railway stations. When going to print, booking online was still not available, only by phone. However, it saves time in looking up different rail networks and ferry companies. Just phone them, and they will link it all up for you, and offer very reasonable prices. It is a UK-based organisation, and so it does not link up with Irish stations, and booking needs to be done in the UK. However, if your journey starts in Ireland, you can still book via SailRail, but you need to allow ten days for the ticket to be posted, and there is an extra charge of £5 for international postage. If you are travelling from Northern Ireland, give it five working days for the ticket to arrive. The other option, if you have friends or family in the UK, is to ask them to pick the ticket up for you at one of SailRail's participating stations, and post it to you. Examples of prices are London Euston to Dublin ferry port £24 single, or Glasgow to Belfast £18 single.

Website: www.sailrail.co.uk
Telephone: From the UK, +44 (0) 8450 755 755, Monday-Friday 8am-8pm, weekends 9am-5pm

Taking the bus

Eurolines
This European-wide coach network is a cheap and efficient way to travel slowly between Ireland and the UK. They offer services to and from various UK cities to Dublin, Belfast and Cork, with connections to many other Irish towns. Their brochure is extremely detailed, giving connection times throughout Ireland. They even tell you the names of the shops or pubs, outside which the bus will stop. One of the biggest advantages of Eurolines is that they take you to the city centre or the port, so no worries about transfers, taxis or trailing luggage.
Website: www.eurolines.com
Telephone: +353 (0) 1 83 66 111 for Republic of Ireland residents or +44 (0) 8705 143219 for UK residents

Ulsterbus
Northern Ireland's extensive coach service provides access to a lot of rural areas, as well as its Goldline service which is an express intercity service. North and East bound services from Belfast depart Laganside Buscentre. South and West bound services depart from Europa Buscentre. Times and fares are available on Translink's website (www.translink.co.uk), an organisation which has integrated Northern Ireland's public transport facilities, and provides information on a one-stop-shop website. Their journey planner is an

excellent way of working out which form of transport you need to take from one place to another. Bicycles are carried free of charge if the bus has a boot and space is available. Fold-up bicycles can be carried at any time on-board the vehicle.

Website: www.translink.co.uk
Telephone: Translink call centre: +44 (0) 28 9066 6630

Bus Eireann

The Republic of Ireland's main coach service offers a good service throughout Ireland. It also has an impressive selection of 'Tourist Passes', such as the Open Road Pass €49 for three day's travel, or the Emerald Card, €248 for eight days' unlimited travel (out of 15 consecutive days). Their best product is the Irish Explorer Bus and Rail, which although pricey, it does cover the whole country for €220, for eight days travel (out of 15 consecutive days). There are half-price tickets for children.

They cannot guarantee it, but if there is enough room they will carry bikes in the luggage compartment. It costs €11 per single journey. Folding bicycles are carried free of charge in the luggage, but they must be in appropriate bags.

Website: www.buseireann.ie
Telephone: +353 (0) 1 836 6111 for travel information from Dublin. All other bus stations are listed on website

The train enters Belfast.

Taking the train

Irish Rail

There is a growing network of trains in Ireland, and a lot of the stock is currently being upgraded. There are two central stations in Dublin; Heuston station which generally serves the West, and Connelly Station, which serves the North and South East. Irish Rail also offers Rail Tours to popular tourist destinations. These can be found at www.railtoursireland.com. Irish Rail is in the process of improving its bicycle facilities, but in general you can take a bicycle (for a charge of €8) on most intercity services, although times are restricted. The most up to date information can be found on the website, but best to check with the railway station. You cannot reserve a bicycle space. They have a concise list of bike hire companies on their website, under 'Company information'. I recommend you check their website for information on line closures before planning any long trips. Another independent and very informative website, set up by Irish rail users, is www.railusers.ie.

Website: www.irishrail.ie
Telephone: +353 (0) 1 8366 222 or Talking Timetable at 1890 77 88 99 (from Republic of Ireland)

Northern Ireland Railways

The rail network in Northern Ireland is still limited, although the two hour cross-border Belfast to Dublin service is excellent and stock is being currently updated on other lines. Within Northern Ireland, the network includes Bangor, Londonderry, Coleraine, Portrush, Portadown, Newry. There are five main stations in Belfast, and services vary out of each. They are Central, Botanic, City Hospital, Gt. Victoria Street and Yorkgate. Price examples are £6.80 return from Belfast to Bangor, and £14 return to Londonderry. If you are between 16-21, you can get a discount card, but there are no family travel card offers.

Website: www.nirailways.co.uk
Telephone: +44 (0) 28 9066 6630

GO SLOW IN THE SOUTH WEST

ecoescapes in this region:

South Reen Farm, Cork
Turn to page 28

Hagal Farm, Cork
Turn to page 30

Whale Watch West Cork, Cork
Turn to page 33

The Mustard Seed at Echo Lodge, Limerick
Turn to page 36

CORK

Places to Eat

Quay Co-op
24 Sullivans Quay, Cork
T: +353 (0) 21 431 7660
W: www.quaycoop.com

In the centre of Cork, the Quay Co-op is a vegetarian restauarant, organic food shop and bakery. Founded in 1982, the shop and restaurant are run as a workers' co-operative which has since then been an important part of the community. The cheery self-service restaurant serves a range of vegan and vegetarian dishes and caters for many dietary requirements. You can take away some organic bread including spelt, soda, cornbread and wholemeal varieties.

Organico
2 Glengarriff Road, Bantry, Cork
T: +353 (0) 27 51391
W: www.organico.ie

The splendid Organico bakery and café is an 'emporium' of good, wholesome and organic food. The staff are brimming with enthusiasm and on hand to take you through their impressive array of produce, including home-baked bread and local cheeses. The café serves filling lunches and fairtrade teas and coffee. Open Monday to Saturday, 9.30am-6pm, you can also stop here to check your email.

Places to Visit

Woodcock Smokery
Skibbereen, Cork
T: +353 (0) 28 36232
W: www.woodcocksmokery.com

Sally Barnes set up this smokery in the 1980s because her husband was a fisherman and there was always too much fish to eat, and not enough money to buy a freezer. So, she tried to find ways to make it last. She went on to create a thriving award-winning business in West Cork, the centre of Irish food artisans. As an active member of Slow Food Ireland, Sally sources all of her wild salmon locally. It is caught in nets at sea by local fishermen, within 9km of the coast. You can order online from her website, and download some of her superb recipes so that you are prepared for when it arrives in the post. Gives a whole new meaning to 'salmon parcels'.

Activities

Sea Kayaking West Cork
T: +353 (0) 86 309 8654
W: www.seakayakingwestcork.com

Choose from a variety of kayaking trips off the Cork coast. For one-day trips, try the seal safari in Glengarriff and enjoy the stunning environment of Bantry Bay. The bay is dotted with small islands and protected by a horseshoe of mountains which give it a unique micro-climate. For longer trips, the company offers adventures to Bere and North Shore islands. Frank Conroy and Victoria Hallam run the trips and ensure that their small groups of paddlers cause minimal disturbance to the wildlife. They can also recommend local accommodation to suit a range of budgets.

Green Wood Chairs

The Wooden House, Rossnagoose,
Skibbereen, Cork
T: *+353 (0)28 21890*
W: *www.greenwoodchairs.com*

Alison Ospina is the craftslady behind Green Wood Chairs. Not only does she create these rustic chairs to sell but she teaches others the craft through her workshops in West Cork. Alison uses locally coppiced unseasoned Hazel as the raw material – a sustainable way to grow and harvest the wood. She also encourages the planting and management of the woodlands which form the backdrop to her courses. Chair-making courses take place over three days, at the end of which, you'll have your very own hand-made creation to sit on.

Hand-crafted chairs at Green Wood Chairs

Places to Stay – Hotels, Self-Catering & B&Bs

Green Lodge

Trawnamadree, Ballylickey, Bantry, Cork
T: *+353 (0) 27 66146*
W: *homepage.eircom.net/~greenlodge*

Green Lodge is a group of self-catering apartments with a special focus on vegan and vegetarian visitors. It's also a welcome stop-off point for walkers and cyclists exploring the Cork countryside. A substantial organic garden provides guests with in-season vegetables, while organic wholefoods and home-baked organic bread is also available. The apartments are set against the striking background of West Cork, surrounded by natural woodland, streams and hills, and are 3km from the coast. Stone circles, standing stones and other historical monuments also dot the local landscape.

Ballymaloe House

Shanagarry, Cork
T: *+353 021 465 2531*
W: *www.ballymaloe.ie*

In rural East Cork, Ballymaloe House is a 400-acre estate and country house hotel. The estate has maintained remnants of the past with its 15th Century Norman Tower and 16th Century gatekeeper's house. Its sympathetic restoration gives the hotel and self-catering cottages a unique edge and the elegant rooms look out onto the gardens which feature an array of colour in the summer months. You might see the odd hen or two which supply fresh eggs for breakfast to go with home-made bread and free-range bacon. Nearby Kenmare Bay supplies the restaurant with fresh shellfish – Ballymaloe's house speciality.

KERRY

Places to Visit

Kerry Alternative Technology

Gortagowan, Sneem, Killarney, Kerry
T: *+353 (0) 64 45563*
W: *www.kerryat.com*

The 40-acre farm at KAT is owned by Bob and Cath Donoghue-Barnes and their two children. It's a self-professed 'rough and ready' place but a charming and interesting one at that. Regular tours of the farm explore its impressive range of renewable technologies like the water and wind turbines. For more in-depth insight, you can also participate in workshops and residential courses or otherwise volunteer on the farm through WWOOF. Basic bunk house facilities are available.

Places to Stay – Hotels, Self-Catering & B&Bs

An Tigh Beag

Glanteenassig, Castlegregory, Kerry
T: *+353 (0)87 779 3126*
W: *www.tighbeag.com*

An Tigh Beag is a self-catering cottage hidden by 17 acres of native woodland near to the Owencashla River. With a waterfall in view from its front door, An Tigh Beag is located amongst some spectacular scenery including lakes, forests, and mountains. This 19th Century cottage has been renovated using traditional materials such as hemp-lined renders, recycled timbers and thermohemp insulation, while the cottage is heated by geothermal heating. Hill walking is available right on the doorstep, with horse-riding, angling and other outdoor activities all within a 6-mile radius.

The Pheonix

Shanahill East, Castlemaine, Kerry

T: *+353 (0) 66 976 6284*

W: *www.thephoenixorganic.com*

On the Dingle Peninsula in County Kerry, Phoenix Farmhouse offers chalet accommodation along side its vegetarian restaurant and organic gardens. The Slieve Mish Mountains are a wonderful backdrop to the Pheonix and help supply the flow of water through the gardens. And likewise the gardens provide home-grown vegetables to the restaurant which serves wholesome dishes like Persian Curry to be washed down with their selection of organic wines.

GO SLOW IN THE SOUTH EAST

ecoescapes in this region:

EcoBooley

Turn to page 39

CARLOW

Places to Stay – Hotels, Self-Catering & B&Bs

Ballin Temple

Ardattin, Carlow

T: *+353 (0) 59 915 5037*

W: *www.ballintemple.com*

The historic cottages at Ballin Temple enjoy stunning views of the Slaney valley out to the Blackstairs mountains in the distance. The cottages are small and intimate with many of the original features intact or sympathetically restored. Guests can explore the ancient woodlands or wander around the organic gardens which supply the farm with produce. Yoga and fishing are also available.

Lorum Old Rectory

Kilgreaney, Bagenalstown, Carlow

T: *+353 (0) 59 977 5282*

W: *www.lorum.com*

At the foot of the Blackstairs Mountains, Lorum Old Rectory is a homely, yet elegant bed and breakfast in County Carlow. The manor house is packed full of old photos and family memorabilia and has views out to the surrounding countryside. The open wood and turf fires are welcome comfort after a long day's walk or cycle. Bobbie, Lorum's hostess, is a talented cook and uses her own home-grown and local organic produce in her dishes. She's also a member of 'Euro-Toques' – a European initiative set up to defend local culinary heritage.

KILLKENNY

Places to Stay – Hotels, Self-Catering & B&Bs

Croan Cottages
Dunnamaggan, Kilkenny
T: *+353 (0) 87 236 8555*
W: *www.croancottages.com*
The self-catering cottages at Croan House are set around a courtyard in the grounds of the historic Croan House in Kilkenny. The land is described as a 'working smallholding' which means that Croan is aiming to become self-sufficient in home-grown produce before long. They have even planted an orchard of apple, pear, plum and cherry trees which incorporates some rare Irish indigenous varieties. The hedgerow and woodland also have an abundance of wild food, so foraging is a regular activity at Croan. All the kitchen vegetable waste is composted and rainwater is harvested to feed the gardens.

TIPPERARY

Places to Stay – Hotels, Self-Catering & B&Bs

Fairymount Farm
Ballingarry, Roscrea, Tipperary
T: *+353 (0) 67 21139*
W: *www.fairymountfarm.com*
Fairymount Farm is home to a trio of self-catering cottages that enjoy a stunning location on the Knochshegowna Hill in County Tipperary. The family-run organic farm has 450 acres to explore including its designated walking trails and private lake. The family also promote better forestry on farms and have spent years protecting the wildlife on their patch. Two of the cottages are modern with pine features while the third is a 200-year-old renovated cottage with heaps of character.

Gortrua Farm
Gortrua, New Inn, Tipperary
T: *+353 (0) 62 722 23*
W: *homepage.eircom.net/~gortruaorganic*
The family in residence at Gortua Farm have succeeded in maintaining organic farming methods since they moved in over 20 years ago. Along with their organically reared herd of cattle, they have restored a traditional cottage, ideal for couples looking for a romantic hideaway. With over 100 acres to play with, the guests at Gortua have

ample opportunity to explore its wild corners and mountain walks in the Galtee range.

The Old Convent
Mount Anglesby, Clogheen, Tipperary
T: *+353 (0) 52 65565*
W: *www.theoldconvent.ie*
The Sisters of Mercy moved out of the Old Convent in 2006 and Dermot and Christine Gannon moved in, to set up their 'gourmet hideaway'. Combining tasteful décor and food with flair, chef Dermot enjoys nothing more than wining and dining his guests. His epic tasting menu is one to be savoured and features delights such as Ballybrado Organic Pork Salad, Rack of Tipperary Lamb and Strawberry Mint Martini. The ingredients are local and organic wherever possible.

Places to Visit

The Apple Farm
Moorstown, Cahir, Tipperary
T: *+353 (0) 52 41459*
W: *www.theapplefarm.com*
The Apple Farm is known across Ireland for its output of delicious fruit. In addition to an array of apple varieties, the farm also grows pears, plums, strawberries and raspberries all of which go into their jams, juices and vinegars which are sold in the farm shop. You can also sleep among the orchards in the farm's camping and caravanning site which is open during the summer months. The showers on the site are heated by solar panelling and there are extensive recycling facilities for campers.

WEXFORD

Places to Stay – Hotels, Self-Catering & B&Bs

Kilmokea Country Manor & Gardens
Great Island, Campile, Wexford
T: *+353 (0) 51 388 109*
W: *www.kilmokea.com*
Kilmokea is an 18th Century rectory on the banks of the River Barrow near Waterford. Décor and furnishings are traditional Georgian, this elegant formality carries on to the outdoors, where a glorious walled garden boasts 130 species of shrubs and trees. This magical horticultural world also houses the kitchen garden, which supports Kilmokea's organic and Slow Food ethos. The non-horticulturists can also enjoy outdoor activities of tennis and croquet. There is also an indoor pool and spa.

Saville House

Enniscorthy, Wexford

T: *+353 (0) 53 923 5252*

W: *www.salvillehouse.com*

Just outside the town of Enniscothy, Saville House bed and breakfast is a small hub of calm. Its Victorian heritage is part of the appeal of the old house which contains five bedrooms, some of which overlook the pristine lawn in the garden. Bring a tennis racket and you can have a game on the lawn too. The food served at Saville House has had some rave reviews not least because of the home-grown produce and carefully sourced fish. There's a Full Irish for breakfast, or otherwise try one of the other imaginative options like rosti and smoked Haddock.

GO SLOW IN THE MIDLANDS

ecoescapes in this region:

Trinity Island Lodge, Cavan

Turn to page 43

The Old Schoolhouse, Cavan

Turn to page 46

Wineport Lodge, Westmeath

Turn to page 49

CAVAN

Places to Eat

MacNean House and Restaurant

Blacklion, Cavan

T: *+353 (0) 71 985 3022*

W: *www.macneanrestaurant.com*

There are two conditions to eat at Macnean House. Book a taxi home as the wine list is irresistible, and book a table well in advance, as this restaurant has won just about every foodie award going. Owner and chef, Neven Maguire, is a major player in promoting sustainability and traceability in food production. Enjoy dishes like Duo of Wild Rabbit – a pie and stuffed saddle, or good old Fillet of Irish Beef.

Activities

Corleggy Cheese School

Belturbet, Cavan

T: *+353 (0) 49 952 2930*

W: *www.corleggy.com*

Take a course in cheese-making at nearby Corleggy Farm. Instead of bringing your own bottle, you bring your own bucket. A bucket, a ladle and an apron are all you need to partake in a day of cheese-making at Corleggy Summer Cheese School. It's a day-long course which sends you back home (with your bucket) and your own one kilo of cows' milk cheese. Courses cost €150, including organic lunch, and wine.

Places to Stay – Hotels, Self-Catering & B&Bs

Sandville House

Ballyconnell, Cavan

T: *+353 (0) 49 952 6297*

W: *homepage.eircom.net/~sandville*

This rural hostel near Ballyconnell is in a converted barn. It is ideal accommodation for cyclists and backpackers visiting County Cavan. There's a cosy living area with turf fire and plenty of open space around the building to explore. The bunkbed dorms range in size and there's a sociable dining area to eat in. The hostel can be booked out by groups of up to 24 people.

LAOIS

Places to Stay – Hotels, Self-Catering & B&Bs

Coolanowle Farmhouse

Ballickmoyler, Carlow

T: *+353 (0) 59 862 5176*

W: *www.coolanowle.com*

An Organic Demonstration Farm for the Department of Agriculture, Coolanowle invites guests to enjoy some rural living in its bed and breakfast farmhouse and self-catering cottage. You're assured of some good home-baking as a guest in the B&B along with simple, traditional rooms. Evening meals consist of organic meat from the farm and Full Irish for breakfast. Guests can enjoy some pampering with a natural spa treatment during their stay which can also be part of a package residential deal.

WESTMEATH

Places to Stay – Hotels, Self-Catering & B&Bs

Cornaher House Organic Farm Bed & Breakfast

Tyrrellspass, Westmeath

T: *+353 (0) 44 23311*

W: *homepage.eircom.net/~westmeath*

Cornaher House is an imposing Georgian manor in County Westmeath to the west of Dublin. Dating back to the 19th Century, the bed and breakfast is full of old-world character with some modern additions. The house is located on an organic working farm of 150 acres where a friendly stock of cattle roam the fields. Guests can also wander through the farm's own grassland, woodland and bogland.

Cornaher House, Westmeath

GO SLOW IN THE EAST

ecoescapes in this region:

The Old Milking Parlour, Wicklow
Turn to page 52

Bellinter House, Meath
Turn to page 55

Cultivate, Dublin
Turn to page 58

DUBLIN

Places to Eat

Eden
Meeting House Square, Temple Bar, Dublin 2
T: *+353 (0) 16 705 372*
W: *www.edenrestaurant.ie*

Owned by the man behind Bellinter House Jay Bourke, the Eden Restaurant in Dublin is one of his city-based ventures. The food is contemporary, with a nod to Irish cuisine, principally through the use of Irish-reared meat. The dinner menu is imaginative and wholesome, with local and traditional flavours. The minimal decor and laid back ambience is popular with locals and visitors alike.

Places to Visit

Enfo
17 St. Andrew Street, Dublin 2
T: *+353 (0) 18 88 2001*
W: *www.enfo.ie*

For information on everything eco and sustainable, the ENFO Centre should be your first port of call. The Centre houses exhibitions on the environment along with extensive resources and publications on sustainability. You can call in to the Centre in Dublin, or otherwise the helpful staff can send out information to you. Topics of interest include climate change, waste management, wildlife and sustainable development.

Activities

Ecocabs
Dublin
W: *www.ecocabs.ie*

As Dublin becomes more and more congested, this company has come up with an ingenious alternative to taxis. They have a fleet of modern passenger tricycles operating a free shuttle service between 10am-7pm, daily, from April to December. Ecocabs benefit from getting sponsorship from companies who want to splash their products all over the vehicle, and you benefit from getting a free ride across town. Operating from designated pick-up points, within a two kilometre radius of O'Connell Bridge.

WICKLOW

Places to Eat

The Strawberry Tree
The Brooklodge & Wells Spa, Macreddin Village, Wicklow
T: *+353 (0) 40 236444*
W: *www.brooklodge.com*

The Strawberry Tree is a certified organic restaurant housed in Brooklodge – a country spa hotel in the Wicklow Valley. The menu in the restaurant uses only organic and wild ingredients that come from the local area and produced by artisan suppliers. The result is a memorable array of flavours from dishes such as the Macreddin Smoked Salmon Rillette, Wild Sorrel and Lemon Dressing. The menu changes regularly with the seasons.

Places to Visit

An Tairseach

Dominican Farm and Ecology Centre,
Wicklow Town, Wicklow

T: *+353 040 461 833*

W: *www.ecocentrewicklow.ie*

The Dominican Sisters established the Dominican Farm and Ecology Centre in 1998 on their 70 acres of land in Wicklow. The farm is organic and biodynamic and home to the Centre for Ecology and Spirituality. Their programme of retreats covers everything from 'Spirituality Through Art' through to 'Growing Organic Vegetables in a Small Garden'. Tours of the farm and Ecology Centre can also be arranged.

Mount Usher Gardens

Ashford, Wicklow

T: *+353 (0) 40 440 205*

W: *www.mountushergardens.ie*

On the banks of the River Vartry, Mount Usher has been designed in the style of celebrated 19th Century garden designer, William Robinson. Equally luscious are the shops and café, most of which are run by Avoca, Ireland's leading provider of gourmet foods, local crafts and designer giftware. This is dangerously delicious credit card territory, as you stock up on everything from funky wellies to takeaway treats. Or just lodge yourself in the garden café and gorge on all things Avoca.

Places to Stay – Hotels, Self-Catering & B&Bs

Brook Lodge Hotel

Macreddin Village, Wicklow

T: *+353 (0) 40 236 444*

W: *www.brooklodge.com*

A self-contained eco hotel, spa, pub and restaurant, the Brook Lodge is an oasis of calm in the Wicklow Valley south of Dublin. The rooms combine tradition with New York style, some of which boast balconies that overlook the village green. The restaurant is certified organic (see the Strawberry Tree above) and brews its own organic lager and stout served in the nearby Actons Pub. There are extensive recycling facilities in the hotel along with their own peat sewage treatment system. The hotel has also commissioned a wood chip plant to provide all the current heat for the building and for the spa and pool.

Brook Lodge, Wicklow

GO SLOW IN THE NORTH WEST

ecoescapes in this region include:

Greenbox

Kingfisher Cycle Trail

Benwiskin Centre, Sligo

Voya Seaweed Baths, Sligo

The Gyreum, Sligo

Coopershill House, Sligo

The Breesy Centre, Donegal

Ard na Breatha, Donegal

Creevy Cooperative, Donegal

Ard Nahoo, Leitrim

Tawnylust, Leitrim

The Organic Centre, Leitrim

Lough Allen Adventure Centre, Leitrim

The Old Rectory, Leitrim

DONEGAL

Activities

Gartan Outdoor Education Centre

Church Hill, Letterkenny, Donegal
T: *+353 (0) 70 4913 7032*
W: *www.gartan.com*

On the shores of Gartan Lough, this activity and education centre is perfectly placed to offer visitors unparalleled access to the outdoors. During the summer months, the Centre runs a sailing, surfing and windsurfing school as well as numerous environmental courses. The recently built Boathouse, provides a base from which to explore the area. It was built with sustainable materials and features a biomass boiler with underfloor heating. Inside there's a small coffee shop with views out over the lake.

Donegal Organic Farm

Doorian, Glenties, Donegal
T: *+353 (0) 74 955 1286*
W: *www.donegalorganic.ie*

The 750 acres of land at Donegal Organic Farm are dedicated to the pursuit of organic and bio-dynamic farming methods. The philosophy behind the farm is to practice sustainable land use, and involve others through farm volunteering and their eco-camp. Camp participants can learn more about farming, forestry and wildlife in this stunning highland location in Donegal. There are also opportunities to go walking, mountaineering and canoeing in the surrounding area. The farm has three holiday flats to rent as well as a number of renewable energy projects on the go including a hydro-electric turbine which powers the underfloor heating of the main farmhouse.

Places to Stay – Hotels, Self-Catering & B&Bs

The Bluestack Centre

Drimarone, Donegal
T: *+353 (0) 74 973 5564*
W: *www.independenthostelguide.com &*
www.donegaltown.ie

A community-run centre in the Bluestack Mountains with a 28-bedroom hostel. There is a family room, dormitory accommodation and an en-suite special needs room, ideal for wheelchair users. The Centre is well-placed for walking on the Bluestack Way, which begins in Donegal Town, and is part of the national Waymarked Way system. The Centre is 3km from the main path of the walk, and

it has its own hill walking group, the Bluestack Ramblers. It is also a popular place for fishermen, heading off to the nearby River Eany in search of trout and salmon.

Rathmullan House

Rathmullan, Donegal
T: *+353 (0) 74 915 8188*
W: *www.rathmullanhouse.com*

Ruthmullan is a country house which exudes taste and character along with its reputation for providing guests with a friendly welcome and smart service. The house enjoys a unique setting that incorporates stately and walled gardens and the pristine Lough Swilly. The Weeping Elm Restaurant has won numerous awards and uses its setting to supply the restaurant. The seaside isn't far away which means fresh fish and seafood are a regular feature on the menu, while specialities like Donegal lamb come from local farms. The organic kitchen garden provides much of the vegetable, fruit and herbs.

LEITRIM

Places to Eat

Clancy's of Glenfarne

Brockagh, Glenfarne, Leitrim
T: *+353 (0) 71 985 3116*
W: *www.clancysofglenfarne.com*

On the main N16 road, Clancy's of Glenfarne serve top breakfasts. If the eight baking bowls on the kitchen table aren't proof enough of the home made bread, the smell will be. Like many Irish restaurants, they subscribe to Bord Bia (The Irish Food Board), ensuring all food products are sourced locally and traceable 'from farm to fork'.

The Riverbank Restaurant

Dromahair, Leitrim, +353 (0) 71 91 64934
W: *www.riverbank-restaurant.com*

Treat yourself to the set menu (one for kids too) at the Riverbank Restaurant, where the chef is a local man who understands the importance of keeping things local. There are numerous meat and fish dishes including Ballotine of Cornfed Chicken and Pan Flashed Turbot. The restaurant is located on the picturesque banks of the Bonet River in Dromahair.

Cedar Surfboards
Mullaun, Manorhamilton, Leitrim
T: *+353 (0) 71 985 5442*
W: *www.cedarsurfboards.com*
Buy an Irish ecofriendly surfboard at Cedar Surfboards. These hollow wooden surfboards, made from cedar strips and epoxy, are works of art. Max, the artisan who makes these beauties told me "We don't build surfboards for winning competitions. We build them for having fun, and getting the most possible pleasure out of life. Our line of boards is based around solid function and enjoyment rather than fashion". Order in advance, so you can pick it up en route to the Donegal or Sligo surf.

SLIGO

Places to Eat

Clevery Mill
Castlebaldwin, Sligo
T: *+353 (0) 71 912 7424*
W: *www.cleverymill.com*
In Castlebaldwin, Clevery Mill is where head chef Diarmuid grows much of the grub himself. The menu changes regularly and includes Filet of Riverstown beef with smoked bacon galette potatoes as well as other locally reared meat. There are also six guest bedrooms in the converted mill if you're planning to stay.

Places to Visit

Sligo Folk Park
Millview House, Riverstown, Sligo
T: *+353 (0) 71 916 5001*
W: *www.sligofolkpark.com*
The Sligo Folk Park is a tiny museum in Riverstown. The folk park is a community-run attraction and provides a glimpse of 19th Century rural and Irish heritage. There is a wonderful museum and exhibition hall where visitors can see one of Ireland's finest collections of agricultural artefacts. There is a pretty fine collection of locally-made cakes on sale in the café too.

Kilcullen Seaweed Baths
Enniscrone, Sligo
T: *+353 (0) 96 36238*
W: *www.kilcullenseaweedbaths.com*
Ireland's oldest seaweed bathhouse, and most fascinating in terms of history, is Kilcullens, at Enniscrone in County Sligo. Opened in 1912, it has been run by the Kilcullen family for five generations. All the original features have been kept, including the Edwardian glazed porcelain baths with the type of solid brass taps which take two hands to creak into position. Even more impressive are the old cedar steam boxes. I closed the lid over my head leaving it to poke through the hole, and pressed the button marked 'Steam'. As my head was not in direct contact with the steam, it felt less oppressive than modern steam rooms enabling you to breathe in the cool air while the rest of your body gets a good old steaming.

Places to Visit

Irish Raptor Research Centre
Ballymote, Sligo
T: *+353 (0) 71 918 9310*
W: *www.eaglesflying.com*
This is Ireland's largest sanctuary for birds of prey and owls. Run mostly by volunteers, this Centre is based in Ballymote, County Sligo. They have daily flying demonstrations, from Easter until early November, where you can see eagles, hawks and falcons free-flying, accompanied by a talk on the conservation of these endangered species. There is also a pet zoo with goats, lambs, donkeys, horses, guinea pigs, rabbits, ferrets and pot-bellied pigs, making this a great family day out.

Following the Mourne Wall, County Down

GO SLOW IN NORTHERN IRELAND

ANTRIM

Activities

Belfast Safaris

331-333 Shankhill Road, Belfast,
Antrim BT13 3AA
T: *+44 028 9031 0610*
W: *www.belfastsafaris.com*

Getting to know a city better requires a certain amount of local knowledge. The walking tours by Belfast Safaris not only display a great deal of insight into the city but get to grips with the issues that affect it. As a social enterprise, they consider that theirs is a role that brings visitors closer to the local population. Walks veer off the beaten track and include themed tours such as 'Natural Belfast' which explores natural environments and how we can better protect them.

Places to Stay – Hotels, Self-Catering & B&Bs

Kinramer Cottage

Rathlin Island, Antrim
T: *+44 (0) 28 2076 3948*
W: *www.antrimcampingbarns.co.uk*

On the 'wild west' of Rathlin Island, Kinramer Cottage is an eco camping barn that offers basic facilities for up to 12 people in two shared dormitories. The interior is bright and cheery, as is the Cottage. The Cottage was converted as part of a sustainable tourism initiative in Northern Ireland and is located on an organic farm on the way to the RSPB seabird viewing point. Guests can use the self-catering kitchen in the Cottage, but don't forget to bring a sleeping bag.

DOWN

Activities

Comber Greenway

W: *www.combergreenway.org.uk*

The Comber Greenway is a new 12km traffic-free section of the National Cycle Network being developed by Sustrans along the old Belfast to Comber railway line. Although many sections are already open to walkers and cyclists, it is due for completion in September 2008. It provides a tranquil green corridor from Comber to East Belfast.

Iron Donkey Bicycle Touring

15 Ballyknockan Road, Saintfield,
Down BT24 7HQ
T: *+44 (0) 28 9081 3200*
W: *www.irondonkey.com*

The Iron Donkey, otherwise known as a bicycle, is the preferred mode of transport for this cycle tour operator. They offer guided and independant cycle tours throughout Ireland taking in stunning scenery on mainly quiet roads. Tours range between 6 and 14 days and there are plenty of refreshment stops along the way in Ireland's finest pubs. In Northern Ireland, tours include the Causeway Coast and Glens of Antrim. A self-guided tour starts at around €495 including accommodation.

Soak Seaweed Baths

5a South Promenade, Newcastle,
Down BT33 0EX
T: *+44 (0) 28 4372 6002*
W: *www.soakseaweedbaths.co.uk*

Soak seaweed baths, in Newcastle, County Down is the latest addition to Irish seaweed centres. Here, you have the added luxury of choosing a CD to be piped to your room, while you bliss out on Bladderwrack. From Summer 2008, they open their own café, SIP, to have a detox drink after your bath, or you can completely crash out after your weed experience, at their self-catering apartment, overlooking the sea, aptly named Snooze.

Places to Stay – Hotels, Self-Catering & B&Bs

Lurganconary Organic Farms

15 Lurganconary Road, Kilkeel,
Down BT34 4LL
T: *+44 (0) 28 3025 4595*
W: *www.lurganconaryfarms.com*

At the foot of the Mourne Mountains, Lurganconary is home to a pair of secluded cottages tucked away on the 100-acre organic farm. Both cottages have surprisingly modern interiors but not without wood-burning stoves in both living rooms. The rest of the heating comes from a geo-thermal system, generating energy from heat below the ground. The farm uses traditional methods such as employing shire horses to clear woodland to help protect vulnerable wildlife from heavy machinery. Part of the farmland has been dedicated to growing willow trees which will be used as another source of green fuel when harvested.

FERMANAGH

Places to Eat

The Cherry Tree
107-109 Main Street, Lisnaskea, Fermanagh
T: +44 (0) 28 6772 1571
W: www.wheresmywheaten.com

Lisnaskea is not really the epicurean centre of Ireland, but Northern Ireland is famous for its selection of breads, and the Cherry Tree is a fantastic home bakery to stock up on soda farls, potato bread, wheaten, scones, pancakes and fruit sodas. This is a family-run business, which prides itself on sourcing as many of its ingredients, including sandwich fillings from its deli counter, in the Fermanagh region.

Places to Visit

Field Studies Centre (FSC)
Derrygonnelly, Fermanagh
T: 144 (0) 28 6864 1673
W: www.field-studies-council.org

The FSC is a UK charity set up to raise awareness of the environment. It has various centres around the UK, and the only one in Ireland is this one in Derrygonnelly, County Fermanagh. The Derrygonnelly Centre lies in the unspoilt West Fermanagh countryside. The River Sillees runs through the Centre's grounds, which is the focal point for many of their workshops, which include family day and residential wildlife and nature courses. Accommodation is also available.

Tickety Moo
Oghill Farm Killadeas, Irvinstown, Fermanagh BT94 1RG
T: +44 (0) 28 6862 8779
W: www.tickety-moo.com

Oghill Farm is the HQ of Ireland's finest and creamiest ice cream, Tickety Moo. If you come at around 5pm, you can watch the impressive herd of Jersey cows being brought in to be milked. They have installed a viewing gallery to encourage consumers to gain a greater understanding of the source of their top-quality ingredients. This is a great family excursion, topped off with a purchase of the final product, which comes in eighteen different flavours. If you are there in summer, go for the Balmy Strawberry. They use Orchard Acre's strawbs and balsamic vinegar.

Places to Stay – Hotels, Self-Catering & B&Bs

Dromard House
Tamlaght, Enniskillen, Fermanagh BT74 4HR
T: +44 (0) 28 6638 7250
W: www.dromardhouse.com

Dromard, meaning 'high ridge' is exactly where you'll find this organic farm and bed and breakfast. On a woodland hilltop, the 180-acre farm is managed by sustainably by the Clive family through wildlife conservation and organic farming methods. The farmhouse B&B uses a woodstove for heating and hot water fuelled by timber obtained by careful woodland management. There is also a self-catering apartment on the farm.

Places to Stay – Campsites & Holiday Parks

Rushin House Caravan Park
Holywell, Belcoo, Fermanagh BT93 5DU
T: +44 (0) 28 6638 6519
W: www.rushinhousecaravanpark.com

Rushin House is on a family farm about a mile from the border town, Belcoo. Despite being only open just over a year, the owners, Cathal and Brenda O'Dolan, have worked hard to create a small caravan park on the raised ground behind their 1870's farmhouse. The O'Dolans built the farmhouse, and are committed to preserving the small piece of natural heritage as best possible. They have a small amount of cattle, and so, just as their visitors are waking up to a day on the lake, Cathal and Brenda might well be out in the fields. Lucky then for the fishermen who could almost throw a line from their beds, as Rushin is right on the shores of Lough Macnean, a wonderful coarse fishing lake for Pike, Perch, Bream, Roach, Hybrid Eels and Brown Trout. Rushin House is also suitable for families, as it is a good safe distance from the road, and with water park facilities just down the road at Corralea Activity Centre. There are only 25 touring pitches, and a small patch of land by the water's edge for tents.

Rushin House Caravan Park

GO SLOW IN THE WEST

ecoescapes in this region:

Gregans Castle Hotel, Clare
Turn to page 128

Cliffs of Moher Visitor Experience, Clare
Turn to page 130

Cnoc Suian, Galway
Turn to page 132

Tír na Fiúse, North Tipperary
Turn to page 135

Ballynahinch Castle, Galway
Turn to page 137

Delphi Adventure Centre, Galway
Turn to page 139

Clare Island Yoga Retreat Centre, Mayo
Turn to page 141

Enniscoe House, Mayo
Turn to page 143

CLARE

Places to Visit

Burren Perfumery
Carron, Clare
T: *+353 (0) 65 708 9102*
W: *www.burrenperfumery.com*
The Burren Perfumery has a tradition of creating products inspired by the landscape and environment that surrounds it. You can take a free tour of the plant-based still and all natural, organic herb garden, with culinary, medicinal and cosmetic herbs on show. This place is an aromatic arena of simple beauty. There is an audiovisual slideshow about the Burren and its flora, after which you can tuck into many of the Perfumery's fine organic cuisine in its tea rooms. Herbal tea is, of course a must. Tea rooms open daily March until September, and at weekends in April.

Centre for Environmental Living and Training (CELT)
East Clare Community Co-op, Main Street, Scariff, Clare
T: *+353 (0) 61 640 765*
W: *www.celtnet.org*
CELT is a charity that helps promote sustainable living through its range of courses and eco-learning holidays. Participants get back to nature through activities such as basket weaving, coppersmithing, wood carving and eco-building. And there's also plenty of opportunities to explore the surrounding countryside between lessons.

The Burren Smokehouse
Lisdoonvarna, Clare
T: *+353 (0) 65 707 4432*
W: *www.burrensmokehouse.ie*
The Burren Smokehouse is in Lisdoonvarna where you can buy a wide array of the most delicious

locally produced delicacies, smoked salmon being the most prolific of course. There is also an audiovisual showing of how salmon is smoked. The craft shop is particularly impressive, with local artisans' works of beauty.

Places to Stay – Hotels, Self-Catering & B&Bs

Berry Lodge

Annagh, Miltown Malbay, Clare
T: *+353 (0) 65 708 7022*
W: *www.berrylodge.com*

Rita Meade is the lady behind Berry Lodge. Her passion for cooking and welcoming guests is apparent throughout her bed and breakfast and cookery school. In the heart of County Clare, Berry Lodge is all about good food available from sea, land and garden in the nearby area. Rita's courses are influenced by the Irish proverb, "Serve fresh young food and mature drink". Her courses include 'Cooking from the Farmers' Market' and 'One Pot Wonders'. For B&B guests, homemade scones are readily available which can be enjoyed in the comfort of the open turf fire.

GALWAY

Places to Visit

Brigit's Garden

Pollagh, Roscahill, Galway
T: *+353 (0) 91 550 905*
W: *www.brigitsgarden.ie*

Spend the day at the stunning Brigit's Garden in Roscahill. There are four gardens created and landscaped to represent the four seasons according to Celtic mythology and tradition of festivals: Samhain, Imbolc, Bealtaine and Lughnasa. This is a place of serenity, spirituality and beauty, where each sculpture, shrub and shrine has been carefully created and installed to represent different aspects of ancient wisdom. Their superb café mirrors the general spiritual ethos of stillness, with a slow (and fine) food policy.

Connemara Smokehouse

Ballyconneely, Galway
T: *+353 (0) 95 23739*
W: *www.smokehouse.ie*

Right on the water's edge at Bunowen Pier in Connemara, this family-run smokehouse has been in the Roberts family for 26 years. It is a great place to stock up on salmon for your trip. This smokehouse also has a house speciality of smoked Irish tuna as

well as smoked cod, kippers and mackerel. The only ingredients used are fish, salt, smoke, herbs, sugar, honey and Irish whiskey. Very pure stuff and, similarly purist, their products cannot be bought in supermarkets, only at the Connemara Smokehouse, by mail order and in a few small selected shops. If you are staying at featured ecoescape Ballynahinch Castle (see pages 137-138), this is only 15km away, and worth the trip.

South Aran Centre

Fishermans Cottage, Inishere,
Aran Islands, Galway
T: *+353 (0) 99 75073*
W: *www.southaran.com*

As well as having one of the most enviable locations in Ireland on the Aran Island of Inishere, this small Centre, with accommodation and organic café, runs courses in traditional skills such as fishing and filleting in July, and fruit picking and pickling in September. They also have kayaks and fishing boats to hire, as well as sea angling holidays. If you need an excuse to visit this extraordinary island, then search no further.

Places to Stay – Hotels, Self-Catering & B&Bs

The Man of Aran Cottage

Kilmurvey, Inis Mór, Aran Islands, Galway
T: *+353 (0) 99 61301*
W: *www.manofarancottage.com*

Inis Mór is the largest of the Aran Isles. Here you'll find the windswept Man of Aran Cottage on the shore of the North Atlantic. Maura and Joe run their B&B and restaurant with a true passion for their location. Joe is an organic farmer and his produce supplies the restaurant with fresh vegetables which Maura duely turns into delicious meals for her guests. Although the island is popular with tourists, cars without permits are forbidden so there's plenty of space to explore with little disturbance.

MAYO

Places to Visit

Ballytoughey Loom

Clare Island, Westport, Mayo
T: *+353 (0) 98 25800*
W: *clareisland.info/loom*

The Ballytoughey Loom is where Beth Moran, the weaver and master craftswoman, has set up her own loom and crafts shop on Clare Island in West

Ireland. If you want the best excuse to stay on the Island, you can take part in one of Beth's weekend or week-long workshops, in spinning, weaving and natural dying. The wool comes from the local sheep and the dyes are made from natural materials from Clare Island.

Kelly Kettle
T: +353 (0) 96 76643
W: www.kellykettle.com

The spiritual home of this ingenious portable kettle is in County Mayo. Invented by the Kelly fishing family, you will make a cup of tea with nothing but a few twigs. If you go fishing on Lough Conn, you can still hire the services of the family's Ghillies, who has the Kelly Kettle close to hand at all times. The additional small cook set transforms it into gas-free cooker too. Order online only.

The famous Kelly Kettle

Places to Stay – Hotels, Self-Catering & B&Bs

Partry House
Partry, Mayo
T: +353 (0) 94 954 3004
W: www.partryhouse.com

Partry is a private estate incorporating an organic farm and historic house. The estate's East Wing and Gate Lodge have been sympathetically restored to offer guests self-catering accommodation with views out to the parkland leading to Lough Carra. The estate is designated a Special Area of

Conservation under the EU directive and has heritage status so conservation is a priority for Partry's owners.

ROSCOMMON

Places to Visit

Lough Key Park & Activity Centre
Rockingham, Boyle, Roscommon
T: +353 (0) 71 967 3122
W: www.loughkey.ie

Lough Key is a forest and activity park with bogs, canals, walking trails, follies and woodland. Wildlife lives in abundance in the park thanks to the density of different tree and wildflower species present. You can explore the park in more detail with an audio trail which points out how humans have changed the landscape through time and will take you to the treetop canopy walk with impressive views over the lake.

GO

Home and Abroad
the new Travel Supplement

Let GO be your travel guide
every weekend

Every Saturday with
THE IRISH TIMES

SUSTAINABLE TOURISM THROUGHOUT IRELAND

Other ecoscapes throughout Ireland:

Irish Farmers' Markets
Turn to page 146

Waymarked Ways of Ireland
Turn to page 149

Coillte

T: *+353 (0) 1 20 11111*
W: *www.coillteoutdoors.ie*

Coillte is a private company set up by the Irish government in 1988 to manage the majority of forests in Ireland. It now owns 70 % of Ireland's forests, with over a million acres of land to its name. It is a profit-making organisation with many forestry-related businesses on its books, all of which not only follow strict codes of practice on sustainability but also are one of Ireland's leading pioneers in corporate social responsibility. In terms of ecoscapes, Coillte's website has invaluable information on all of its forest parks, a concise breakdown of recreation areas and activites in each county of the Republic of Ireland. See www.coillte.ie for details. However, its consumer website has up to date information on all forest-related leisure activities, and gives useful information on Leave No Trace practices, mountain bike tracks, walking events, and family days out.

Environment & Heritage Service
W: *www.ehsni.gov.uk*

Civil servants don't always get the good press they deserve, but there are 700 of them in the EHS, an agency within the Department of the Environment, for whom the aim is "to protect, conserve and promote our natural environment and built heritage for the benefit of present and future generations." Their staff has a wide variety of skills and their website is extremely informative about Northern Ireland's natural and cultural heritage. This includes information on the proposed national park in the Mournes region, Northern Ireland's maritime heritage such as forts or shipwrecks, as well as a detailed list of all protected areas throughout Northern Ireland.

Euro Toques Ireland
W: *www.eurotoquesirl.org*

Euro-Toques is a European Community of Cooks, and Euro-Toques Ireland has an impressive and ever-growing list of members. The organisation's main aim is to protect European Culinary Heritage in each of its member countries. They do this by training their members, hotels, restaurants and cafes to use artisan producers, source locally and in season. They have a free booklet of all their members in Ireland available from their website, and worth getting before you holiday in Ireland.

Fairtrade Ireland
Carmichael House, North Brunswick Street, Dublin 7
T: *+353 (0) 1 475 3515*
W: *www.fairtrade.ie*

The fairtrade movement is growing in Ireland, and there are 61 towns, at the time of going to press, which have been awarded Fairtrade Town status. These towns have achieved many goals, under the guidance of their town Council. They ensure that a range of fairtrade products is available in the towns' shops, supermarkets, local cafes, restaurants, and hotels. They also work with the town's main businesses, churches and schools, to coordinate greater usage of fairtrade products.

Féile Bia
T: *+353 (0) 16 685 155*
W: *www.bordbia.ie*

This is an excellent consumer programme set up by Bord Bia, Ireland's national food board. It was developed in response to growing demands for information when eating out on food prouduction standards and traceabililty, or "from farm to fork". The 1,500 members, including restaurants, cafés and hotels, commit to, where possible, sourcing fresh, local food. They aim to promote small artisan producers, and highlight the suppliers on menus. Members source meat and eggs from suppliers approved under recognised Quality Assurance Schemes, or from small scale suppliers with appropriate regulatory approval, including butchers. Look for the Féile Bia outdoor plaque and window stickers.

Irish Organic Farmers & Growers Association

Main Street, Newtownforbes

T: *+353 (0) 43 42495*

W: *www.iofga.org*

The Irish Organic Farmers and Growers Association certifies organic food and products throughout Ireland. So to make sure your breakfast really is organic, look for their logo which ensures rigorous organic production and food processing standards. There are now over 1,000 farmers in Ireland registered as organic equating to over 39,000 hectares of organically farmed land.

Irish Peatland Conservation Society

Bog of Allen Nature Centre, Lullymore, Rathangan, Kildare

T: *+353 (0) 45 860 133*

W: *www.ipcc.ie*

This Irish charity was set up 25 years ago to protect the country's precious bogland. It has an active group of volunteers who take on a variety of tasks such as running the Bog of Allen Nature Centre, bog conservation work, and fundraising. Take a walk on some of the bogs mentioned in ecoescape, such as at Cnoc Suain or Tir na Fúise, and you will get a good idea of what keeps this organisation focussed and determined to protect this valuable part of Ireland's heritage. The IPCC website is a font of information on events, such as the Heritage Week with Volunteer Days at Lodge Bog, County Kildare.

Leave No Trace Ireland

T: *+44 (0) 289030 3938*

W: *www.leavenotraceireland.org*

Leave No Trace aims to help those who love the outdoors to protect it through raising awareness of simple practices that keep the environment as beautiful as people find it. The organisation helps protect Ireland's countryside against dangers such as litter, disturbance to vegetation, water pollution, wildlife, livestock and people. Leave No Trace promotes and inspires responsible outdoor recreation through education, research and partnerships.

Railtours Ireland

Railtours Desk, Dublin Tourism Centre, Suffolk Street, Dublin 2

T: *+353 (0) 1 856 0045*

W: *www.railtoursireland.com*

Offering rail tours of Ireland and Northern Ireland starting and ending in Dublin, Rail Tours Ireland has a wide choice of itineraries to help you see more of the country by train. The tours range from one to six days and include rail travel and accommodation. The four-day Grand Atlantic Tour takes in the southern and western coastal regions, with fabulous seascapes and mountain scenery to enjoy along the way.

Slow Food Ireland

W: *www.slowfoodireland.com*

The Slow Food Movement is extremely well-established in Ireland, and several books have recently been written on the subject. These include The Irish Farmers Market Cook Book by Clodagh McKenna, and The Creators, Individuals on Irish Food, by Dianne Curtin. Luckily, there is still not the proliferation of supermarkets in Ireland as in other parts of Europe. Most towns still have a butcher or baker, and it is always worth asking your host to recommend one. For up to date information on Slow Food events around Ireland, their website opens up a whole world of food festivals, smokeries, cheesemakers, butchers and fruit growers.

Sustainable Tourism Ireland

Cultivate Centre, 15-19 Essex Street West, Dublin

W: *www.sustourism.ie*

Founded in 2006, this organisation campaigns for sustainability within the Irish tourism sector. It aims to support and encourage anyone involved in tourism, visitors, providers and tour operators, towards achieving sustainable tourism practices. Such as ensuring minimal environmental impact, respecting and supporting local cultures and traditions, and striving to help local residents gain from tourism income. Although still at the early stages of its development, the volunteers who run this organisation are committed devotees of the sustainable tourism movement, and they promote several excellent tourism providers on their website.

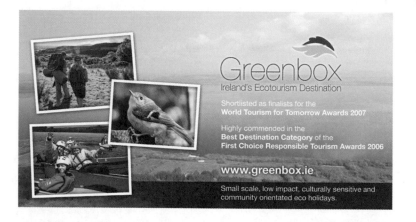

Sustrans Ireland

Marquis Building, 89-91 Adelaide Street,
Belfast, Antrim BT2 8FE

T: *+44 (0) 28 9043 4569*

W: *www.sustrans.org.uk*

Undoubtedly a major force behind the recent 'velorution', Sustrans has been getting people on their bicycles since 1977. The ultimate no-carbon transport option, cycling is fast becoming as much a part of people's holiday plans as their daily school or work commute. Sustrans is responsible for the 12,000 mile long National Cycle Network – a criss-crossing of safe and attractive routes along which to cycle and walk throughout the UK. The routes are numbered and maps are available to help navigate the journey.

Tourism Concern

Stapleton House, 277-281 Holloway Road,
London N7 8HN

T: *+44 (0) 20 7133 3330*

W: *www.tourismconcern.org.uk*

Tourism doesn't always benefit communities around the world. Sometimes our holidays can in fact accentuate poverty in certain countries. Tourism Concern helps address these issues and look for ways to make the tourism industry fairer for people living in holiday destinations. Although Tourism Concern on the whole deals with issues overseas, their campaigns can also relate to tourism structures closer to home.

Waterways Ireland

5/7 Belmore Street, Enniskillen,
Fermanagh BT74 6AA

T: *+44 (0) 28 6632 3004*

W: *www.waterwaysireland.org*

Waterways Ireland is a cross-border organisation, although not surprising as its remit is to manage and maintain the inland waterway system in Ireland, where political borders are pretty much irrelevant. These are navigable waterways and, therefore, particularly of interest for leisure pursuits such as sailing, cruising and angling, as well as walking or cycling on towpaths. Their website has excellent maps of each of their seven waterways, the Erne System, the Grand Canal, the Lower Bann, the Royal, the Shannon-Erne Waterway, Barrow Navigation, and the Shannon Navigation. They also have details of ongoing activities on the waterways, as well as brochures to download such as "A taste of the Waterways", with details of places to eat and drink by the water.

Worldwide Opportunities on Organic Farms (WWOOF)

T: *+44 (0) 1273 476 286*

W: *www.wwoof.org.uk*

The UK and Northern Ireland branch of WWOOF offers UK residents and non-residents the chance to get their hands dirty and work on an organic farm. You'll be fed and watered in return for your hard labour which could involve anything from digging up vegetables and hedgelaying to building and bread-making. Be prepared to work hard and learn some new skills while enjoying being out in the natural environment.

Index

Acknowledgements

With love and thanks, always, to my beloved husband, Brian Brady, and sons, Louis and Hugo. Coming home is always the best bit.

Another personal thank you to my parents, June and Desmond. Mum for putting me on a train out of Belfast when I was eighteen to discover the world. Dad, for teaching me to keep coming home. Because nothing beats listening to Elgar on Errigal.

There are so many people to thank, not least the people I met on my travels in Ireland. I hope I have mentioned most of them in the book. Behind the scenes, a big thanks to all these people, who have put up with my far-too-frequent appearance in their inboxes.

Laura Burgess

Mary Mulvey

Paul McDermott

Debbie Hindle

Kath Freer

Richard Hammond

Miriam Donohue

Marianne Saunders

John Gormley

John Kelly

Hilary Finlay

Jay Bourke

Nuala Ryan

Joanne O'Connor

Linda Moore

Gavin Markham

Terence Cunningham

Elaine Jackson

Martina McCotter

Philip Lowery

Rory Matthews

Paddy Matthews

Jim Rowe

Vanessa Schotes

Joanne Bissett

Barbara Tomasella

Frances Tuke

Sheelagh Wright

Nora Brady

Rosemary and Kieran Phelan

Sean and Eva Brady

Suzanne Brown and Brian Kinsella

Dave Suttle

Meridian Primary School

Freda Palmer

Responsible escapism notes

Get more ecoescapes . . .

Copies of our books and guides can be purchased online at
www.greenguide.co.uk or you can usually find them in bookshops,
independent retailers and organic and wholefood stores. If you need help
finding a local store stocking our books please call us on +44 (0) 1945 461 452
or email the publisher via **publisher@greenguide.co.uk**

Our titles include:
ecoescapes

ecoescape: United Kingdom £8.99
ISBN: 978-1-905731-40-4

ecoescape: Ireland (May 2008) £8.99
ISBN: 978-1-905731-29-9

Green Guide – *the directory for planet-friendly living*
The Green Guide is a series of books and directories focusing on green and
natural products, services and organisations, supported by a comprehensive website and
occasional magazine. Find out more at www.greenguide.co.uk

Green Guide Essentials £6.99
ISBN: 978-1-905731-01-5

The Green Guide to a Greener Wedding £8.99
ISBN: 978-1-905731-49-7

The Green Guide for London 2008 £12.99
ISBN: 978-1-905731-31-2

The Green Guide to a Greener Home £8.99
ISBN: 978-1-905731-50-3

The Green Guide for Scotland £12.99
ISBN: 978-1-905731-32-9

The Green Guide for Wales £12.99
ISBN: 978-1-905731-36-7

You can also find the Pocket Green Guides for England, Scotland
and Wales on the website.

For retailers & wholesalers
Our books are distributed by **Vine House Distribution Ltd**
The Old Mill House, Mill Lane, Uckfield, East Sussex TN22 5AA
t: +44 (0) 1825 767 396
e: sales@vinehouseuk.co.uk